Pompeii

The Tragic Eruption of Mount Vesuvius

(A History of the City and the Eruption of Mount Vesuvius)

Crystel Corkery

Published By **Ryan Princeton**

Crystel Corkery

All Rights Reserved

Pompeii: The Tragic Eruption of Mount Vesuvius (A History of the City and the Eruption of Mount Vesuvius)

ISBN 978-1-77485-914-8

No part of this guidebook shall be reproduced in any form without permission in writing from the publisher except in the case of brief quotations embodied in critical articles or reviews.

Legal & Disclaimer

The information contained in this ebook is not designed to replace or take the place of any form of medicine or professional medical advice. The information in this ebook has been provided for educational & entertainment purposes only.

The information contained in this book has been compiled from sources deemed reliable, and it is accurate to the best of the Author's knowledge; however, the Author cannot guarantee its accuracy and validity and cannot be held liable for any errors or omissions. Changes are periodically made to this book. You must consult your doctor or get professional medical advice before using any of the suggested remedies, techniques, or information in this book.

Upon using the information contained in this book, you agree to hold harmless the Author from and against any damages, costs, and expenses, including any legal fees potentially resulting from the application of any of the information provided by this guide. This disclaimer applies to any damages or injury caused by the use and application, whether directly or indirectly, of any advice or information presented, whether for breach of contract, tort, negligence, personal injury, criminal intent, or under any other cause of action.

You agree to accept all risks of using the information presented inside this book. You need to consult a professional medical practitioner in order to ensure you are both able and healthy enough to participate in this program.

Table Of Contents

Chapter 1: How To Get To Pompeii Using Any Means Of Transportation And At Every Cost! 1

Chapter 2: Continue With The Big Palaestra 32

Chapter 3: The Forum Of Pompeii, The Area In Which Everything Takes Place ... 48

Chapter 4: What Should You Do After Pompeii When You Have A Half Day Off 55

Chapter 5: Oplontis And The Villa Of Poppea... 78

Chapter 6: The Inside Approach To The East 91

Chapter 7: Southern Water Sides 114

Chapter 8: The Forum 126

Chapter 9: The Northwest Sector 142

Chapter 10: The North-Central Sector .. 166

Chapter 1: How To Get To Pompeii Using Any Means Of Transportation And At Every Cost!

Pompeii is among the most loved cities in our gorgeous Italy and is adored by visitors from all over the world.

In 2016 3.209.089 visitors were attracted to in the Ruins in Pompeii. They visited the site to see the remains of an ancient civilization, to think and imagine a time which has gone by and to marvel at the splendor of the majesty of Mount Vesuvius.

Pompeii was discovered around 2000 years ago and its existence as we know it was ended in the year 79 a.D.

A modern and beautiful civilization lived in these regions and it's tragic demise provided us with a unique record of the world's ancient times.

To visit the renowned Archaeological Site, you must arrive at the city of Pompeii situated in the south of Italy located within the Province of Naples.

The journey to Pompeii isn't difficult since Pompeii is in close proximity to other major Italian cities and is accessible by all means of transportation.

In addition, traveling to Pompeii from other countries is effortless and simple because of the nearby Naples international airport that allows connections to Europe, USA and many other countries around the world.

Here are the best ways to reach Pompeii

* Airplane

* Train

* Car

* Bus

* Ship

* On the foot

How to get in Pompeii via Airplane

The option of arriving to Pompeii via plane is the most efficient option for those who are trying to get there from afar.

The nearest airport is the one located in Naples International Airport of Ugo Niutta, Capodichino. It is connected to the major capital cities of Europe and, more than all, during specific seasons open drafts, as well as certain countries outside Europe.

The airport in Naples is the main port of call for numerous companies like Alitalia or Meridiana as well as several of the well-known low-cost businesses such as Easyjet, Volotea and Ryanair There are additionally charter plans and seasonal flights.

Capodichino is the most important airport in southern Italy and from it, numerous flights to major European destinations are able to arrive and depart and depart to and from the United States and sometimes even to Russia.

After you have departed from Naples I recommend you visit the EPT tourist office situated in the arrivals section that is accessible from 7am until 8 pm. There you can get details and suggestions for your next visit to Pompeii.

In the terminal, you will also access a variety of services , including ATM, currency exchange cars, bar, restaurants and other shops.

Capodichino International Airport is a contemporary and comfortable structure which welcomes travelers in a very pleasant manner and offers excellent connections to Naples, the Naples city Naples and its surrounding.

Every 20 minutes, there's an express bus that departs at Naples Airport and linking to the city's centre. From where you'll be able to carry on on your way and arrive in no time at Pompeii.

With the help of Alibus it is possible to reach Napoli's Central Station of Napoli Piazza Garibaldi in just 20 minutes by a safe and comfortable bus that costs 4 euros. On the same route as your Central Station, you can go on to Molo Beverello, from where you can embark on small cruises as well as excursions on islands like Capri, Ischia or Procida. You can purchase tickets on board for the trip without any additional cost.

From Naples airport, you can take S3 bus from the airport. S3 bus to reach the city's centre for 150 euros.

In contrast to the bus that travels on the same route, this vehicle makes many stops and is able to travel for longer time to travel.

There is also the option of traveling to Pompeii directly via taxi, making sure to pick white cars that have permits and fares evident. Due to certain taxi companies, you can arrive in the middle of Naples at around 40 euros in cash and for Pompeii the prices are higher.

You may also hire an automobile to travel to Pompeii. In the Naples Capodichino airport there are the most popular short-term rental businesses and you can choose an NCC service that is actually a hiring a car with a driver. When you arrive to Napoli city centre Napoli city Centre it is essential to determine the best way to get to Pompeii.

Here are the options.

Are you prepared?

Trains can take you to Pompeii via train

To travel to Pompeii via train, most of the time you need to first arrive at Naples Central Station. Naples Central Station and take advantage of the local train.

For instance, if you're booking a speedy train like Italo, FrecciaRossa Trenitalia and Italo the trip will finish in Naples Central Station.

In any case , I advise to think about whether you are from the North like Rome or Florence or Florence, and also the possibility of a train route that will end in Pompeii. You'll need to pick the route that takes you towards Naples but then continues through Calabria to reach destinations farther south than Campania. This way you'll be able to avoid staying in Naples and traveling to Pompeii straight by train from the city of departure.

If you're from the South However, chances are that trains going to Naples offer a stop at Pompeii. Be aware that Pompeii is situated more to the than a few miles to the south than Naples which means that it isn't the case that you have to travel in Naples however you could stop directly in Pompeii when traveling via Trenitalia.

Train from Naples to Pompeii via train

When you arrive to Naples Central Station Piazza Garibaldi you have several ways to reach your destination and begin the tour through the Ruins.

In the following paragraphs I will outline the different options however, don't worryabout it, at the conclusion of this chapter, you'll get my final, sage advice that includes a clear description of the expenses required.

The most secure and simple method of getting between Naples to Pompeii via train is to take trains like the Campania Express tourist train, an express train that connects Naples, Herculaneum, Oplontis, Pompeii and Sorrento.

It's the new generation Metrostar service, operating from April 15 until October 15 and has the shortest and fastest route. The route in Naples, Campania Express only stops at Porta Nolana and Piazza Garibaldi Then it stop within Pompeii, Oplonti and Herculaneum Ruins.

In just 30 minutes, you'll be able to get to Pompeii from Naples The cost of the ticket is 6 euros one-way travel or 11 euros for return.

You can view times and schedules online, as well as purchase tickets Campania Express.

The station of arrival will be Pompei Villa Misteri therefore, you'll have access to the site at the entry point of Porta Marina.

If you are traveling in less popular times I believe that's the best option, this option isn't readily available.

Additionally there is the fact that at Naples central station, you are able to reach Pompeii via Trenitalia train. The train's station that arrives is located near Pompeii's Shrine of Our Lady of Pompeii.

Travel time to Naples is not more than 50 minutes, and the ticket is priced at 3 euros.

The most frequently used and most affordable train to travel from Pompeii will be Circumvesuviana which is the local train which links all vesuvian cities.

In the direction of Naples central station following this line " Napoli - Sorrento" you can stop at Pompei Scavi at the same station on the Campania Express, at the lesser cost of 320 euros per trip and with a traveling for approximately 40 minutes.

This is the most recommended advice , but not the most efficient one.

Here I am going to offer you an alternative for the best option.

If you're planning to reach Pompeii from Naples via it's Circumvesuviana train would suggest you use the Napoli-Poggiomarino train line and arrive near Pompei Santuario, where, following a must-see visit for Pompeii's Shrine of the Madonna of Pompeii it is capable of catching up by a stroll through the new city. the earnings of Piazza Anfiteatro, which is located in and the Ruins from Pompeii.

The price is 320 euros and within 40 minutes you'll reach your destination.

Here are the main reasons for my recommendation:

* First this line of railway is not as frequented by travelers, making it less busy.

You might think that during periods with the highest affluence, there are many visitors every day, who arrive to Pompeii via train, causing congestion and making travel uncomfortable.

* The price for the tickets is close to one-third of that cost of Campania Express one.

If you begin your journey starting from Piazza Anfiteatro, you'll be able to take the most efficient way if you've got a couple of hours and want to explore as much as you can.

The Tour to see Pompeii's Ruins of Pompeii The tour, which I'll offer in the following chapters, is perfect option for those with very little time. In fact, it will give you a preview of about 2 hours.

It begins at the entrance of Piazza Anfiteatro. It ends at the point of income for Porta Marina.

After an exit point, passengers are able to get on the Circumvesuviana train once more, this time from the nearby station in Pompei Scavi, and carry along with your journey to other places.

In the end, if your route to Pompeii is to arrive at Naples before continuing by train to Pompeii for a price of 6,40 Euros, I'd recommend using the Circumvesuviana line Napoli-Poggiomarino. Pompei Santuario stop.

Take into consideration that a visit to Pompeii's ruins Pompeii and train travel, should require approximately 4/5 hours. and then check the timetables of trains to figure out the exact timing and, in general, the trains will run that runs every forty minutes.

How do I get there by car

If you're planning to reach Pompeii by car , you're in the right spot.

The simplest route is to travel on the A3 Napoli-Salerno motorway. It is directly linked with the A1 motorway that comes from Rome or Northern Italy.

Exit to the exit is Pompei Ovest. The cost for exiting tolls from Napoli will be 2 Euros. The time to travel by car from Naples is about 20 minutes with no traffic.

If you are coming to south of the South (Salerno) take the leave at Pompei Est Also, is the cost for the toll. It is 2 euros, to payable in Nocera.

If you are arriving at Pompeii with your car You will have locate a parking space that is either a paid parking in the public area that has blue stripes, or a comfy and safe private parking that is situated near the entrance of the archeological site.

Parking on the blue line on the sidewalks and in other areas will cost you 0,50 euro within the first thirty minutes, and 2 euros in the following hours. You have to display the ticket on the dashboard to pay beforehand at parking machines located close by. To print the ticket at the parking meters, you must indicate the that parking space on the road on which you parking.

Thus whenever you park, look for the number on the blue line and then put it into the parking meters before paying for the fee. It accepts only euros in coins.

Naturally, if you choose this option for parking your vehicle, you'll be required to plan ahead the timing of the break.

I'll be honest with you: I've never chosen this option because I personally would not want to be under the stress of the deadline for the ticket, and also the possibility of paying an amount of money.

On holidays, I like to be able to relax and not worry!

Aren't you?

It is possible to choose an easier solution.

Private parking that will show the cost at the time of exit, by calculating the amount on the basis of the time you've reserved.

Just a short distance from Piazza Anfiteatro, is Piazza Immacolata where you will find the parking that you need!

The price is 150 euros for an hour. it's applicable for cars and motorcycles.

If you're travelling in camping or caravan, you will only have the option of private parking. In this scenario, the cost is 2 euros per hour.

Here is the address of Google Maps in order to catch up

The parking spaces in cities are secure but I advise that you do not keep valuable items in your vehicle.

You will never know.(-)

Reach Pompeii via other means

How do I get to Pompeii via bus

Another option to reach Pompeii is to travel by efficient bus.

With the help of a variety of transport companies, it's easy to get to Pompeii via bus.

For instance, Flixbus offers excursions to Pompeii beginning from the major Italian cities, and often it's quite affordable.

If Flixbus provides the direct route however, it's also the case that other bus operators offer routes to Naples however, you are able to travel from Naples by using the transport options that I have suggested on the previous sections.

Another option, and a popular alternative, is to travel to Pompeii via an excursion on a private bus. In this instance the bus company would have pay a fee to get into Pompeii, as per the RTZs.

How do I get to Pompeii by sea

Naples as well as Salerno Are two most popular cruise ship ports of call within Salerno and Naples, two of the major cruise ship ports that are located in Mediterranean Sea. Many cruise passengers opt to visit the ruins , or attending celebrations of the Catholic faith in the gorgeous town of Pompeii.

In Molo Beverello in Naples, and also at the Port of Salerno It's not difficult to locate companies that organize direct transfers to Pompeii.

Additionally, just outside the ports of Naples you can find the bus that will take your to central station located in Piazza Garibaldi.

It is possible to take the bus 151, which within just 20 mins can get you there, or you can take the Alibus departing from the station for maritime vessels.

Here's a download link for an app that is convenient to use. You can see the timetables

In the direction of Pompeii

It is possible to reach Pompeii through other ways Naturally!

People come here on motorbike, caravan or bicycle or on foot. It's not that weird.

It is believed that the pilgrimage of Pompeii includes hundreds of pilgrims during the year.

From Naples as well as different cities within Campania and other cities in Campania, after walking for miles on foot, the pilgrims of Our Lady of Pompeii arrive at the most significant rituals of worship.

In particular, during May in a manner, at the time of the end month of Marian month and the main roads leading to Pompeii are filled with throngs of pilgrims en route toward the holy shrine.

Maths and the latest advice

If you're wondering which you should pick between those I've offered, I'll give you some other options that will help you in the decision.

To reach Pompeii wherever around the globe, Naples is the first flag that will be pointing you to your way.

The only exception is if you are coming from southern Italy via car or train, it would not be required to travel to Naples as it is farther in the northern part of Italy than Pompeii.

You can make a reservation for an air trip to any Italian city, and when you get a good deal, you could pay for your return flight under 100 euro.

When you arrive you arrive in Naples I would suggest that you take public transport. I would recommend the following alternative: the Circumvesuviana Train, for less than 7 euro you will be able to travel on an A/R.

I recommend you to explore the remains in Pompeii during the day, particularly in hot weather during which walking in the sun is exhausting.

You'll have accept a short walk of 2-3 hours, however, the sunset colors are stunning.

If you are traveling your bulky luggage, you can store them in the luggage storage at Naples station. It'll cost you around 5 euros for each luggage for the duration of a half day.

Trolleys, backpacks and smaller bags may also be dropped off at the free deposit point at the entrance to the archeological site.

The only drawback of this method is that you need to enter and exit the same door in order to take your luggage, and the way is double.

The entrance fee for the ruin is thirteen euros for each person (from Apr.1 1st, 2018 the price will rise up to $15 p.p.) It is recommended to purchase the tickets online to avoid waiting in line which can be very long.

In the end, I'll take care of the math for you. I have excluded here the excursion to Naples as it could provide an excessive amount of options.

With public transportation, you can get to Pompeii ruin in a DIY manner at a cost of around 20 euros for a person, which includes transportation as well as admission tickets.

This is the most affordable option.

If you're looking for a more comfortable travelexperience, and you don't like the crowds of trains, where it is humid and there's the absence of air conditioner, then you could take a taxi, but you should be aware that it will cost at least 100 euros.

It is not possible to give a comprehensive choice.

I'm not sure of your preferences, and more importantly I'm not sure what your travel plan is planned, but my goal is to assist you to discover my area with its wealth of treasures to find. This is why I'll give you the opportunity to reach me for further suggestions to help you plan your trip.

As the subject of the mail send "Maria I'd like to have some more suggestions on how to reach Pompeii".

We've explored all the options to reach Pompeii Your backpack is packed and you've in the middle of the path with your ticket to the entrance.

It's time to embark on this thrilling adventure and discover all the splendor of this fascinating city, which was submerged in the ashes of Mount Vesuvius more than 2000 years ago. It was then discovered thanks to archaeological excavations.

Well...ready?

Follow me, and I'll guide you in by my hand.

There are many ways to take to get to Pompeii You can find a variety of them in any guidebook, however this one I'll recommend to you is the easiest in case you've got a short amount of time and you're not wanting to be missing the most important sights to see.

In fact, I've designed for you a route that allows you to traverse the entire archaeological site within about two hours, and you'll get to see every important spot in the town.

It's a trek you can finish in two hours. You will have to take the moderate route but having the chance of remaining at the top of the list of important points, or, if you have time, complete each stage without any issues.

It's the preferred route picked by the top tour guides to take guests for private tour tours.

In this regard...if you truly want to experience an unforgettable and unforgettable experience I would suggest that you take a private tour to experience the city. It's the most efficient method to explore the city. It's a mistake.

It's a while... We'll try to figure out what you're thinking about...

"Dear Maria, I'm reading your book because I'm headed to an unpaid and self-organized tour of Pompeii So, why are you now recommending me to take a trip with private tour guides?"

You're absolutely right. You're an organized traveler, and I'm with you!

There's nothing better than discovering the unknown than by exploring it on your own and getting completely lost, taking in every little corner, while trying to imagine the tale it is telling.

If you have the time to travel, it's always wonderful but Pompeii is so full of attractions and discover that a full week of exploration would not be enough!

Through an organized tour, you will take a brief but intense tour that covers the most significant social, historical, and cultural aspects of the early Pompeiians living.

If that's the case do not take the first tour you find on the internet or you'll get a suggestion everywhere along your route to Pompeii.

You must choose an experienced tour guide who's foremost enthusiastic about the archeological site, who is aware of every little bit of background of Pompeii and who is competent of engaging and leading you on this thrilling trip by sharing stories and anecdotes that have been handed down over 2000 years.

I'm able to recommend my best friends who perform this work with passion and enthusiasm , and who, in addition, were born and raised in Pompeii and are in a deep and enduring relationship with the city.

I'll introduce them through some interviews I'll share here on my site.

However, if the purpose of your trip to Pompeii is to simply add an additional "flag" to Tripadvisor and you want to add another "flag" to your trip, then just ignore this advice.

The cost of the guided tour isn't within your budget?

Do not worry If this is the case, you only need to adhere to the steps I have laid out for you and get ready to take in all the feelings that this location will bring to you.

It can be beneficial to prepare for your trip by reading a great book that will help you understand the most significant historic and cultural aspect in the area.

Stop chatting... We'll get going.

Here's the 11 step tour to discover the most intriguing places in Pompeii, the Ruins of Pompeii which you'll get to explore in just a few hours.

First...

...let's take a look at the cast of Pompeii.

#00 Let's begin at Amphitheater Square

If you've followed my tips for getting to Pompeii You're in the middle of the Amphitheatre Gate. This is where we begin our journey with a straightforward route that allows you to explore the best important sites in the shortest amount of time.

From the Amphitheatre Gate, you can join various tracks. You may choose to follow the steps step-by-step for each stage of the track I mapped out for you, or leave your own inspiration to guide you.

You can alter your plans at any time by making a few alterations, particularly when the queue at the entry point of the monuments I suggest is long enough (taking too long) or if domus aren't accessible to visitors during the same day.

Are you afraid of getting lost?

Relax since thanks to the work of the Supervisory Authority it's easy to find your way around the city of Pompeii. Just follow the directions which are located near the crossroads.

Did you get the map on the way to the gate?

It's very helpful!

Additionally, I have made a thorough sketch of the route I had planned.

One of the most frequently asked questions that I answer on this blog frequently: "Where's dead people of Pompeii?"

You've probably read about how Giuseppe Fioretti, the most prominent archeologist working in the excavations at Pompeii provided us with the chance to understand the human face of the tragic suffering of those who were victims of the eruption that devastated Pompeii, Ercolaneum and Stabiae.

Utilizing the technology of plaster casts, he revealed their bodies. residents of Pompeii which were discovered in the same spot they were at the time of the pain that came just before the end of the day, and before being buried beneath feet of ash.

In a steel structure located in the main entrance hall just in front of the ticket counter where you can see the statues of Pompeii. Children, women, and men stood up and hugged each other to protect one another from the threat of death.

The structure is now closed, and the 20 castings can be seen only from outside, however taking a peek will cause you to get goose bumps and you'll realize that this isn't art, but the reality of a horrible event that occurred in the year 79 b.C.

#001 Necropolis of Nocera Gate

There was a strong emotion that you felt Aren't you?

After that, you can cross the gate and you'll be able to begin your journey into the site of the ancients.

Wait a moment...

If you're required to use the toilet, take advantage of them now. They are just inside, just to the right of the entryway... and you'll be at ease to begin.

The first step will take visitors to the Necropolis at Nocera Gate.

If you've arrived at Amphitheatre street, you'll see on your left an escalator that takes you to a place with little traffic, but is extremely important.

The Necropolis of Nocera Gate, that would be the actual "cemetery" is home to monuments and structures that display the funerary architecture that was prevalent in the time.

Particularly, there is a structure dating to the Tiberian period, which dates from 14 to 37 a.D. It was built by one of the families of a priestess from Venus, Eumachia.

Its distinctive feature is its high terrace, also known as the Esedra, which has the burial chamber as well as a fence in the rear.

This is a gorgeous concrete work completely covered in Tuff from Nocera and, in the nook are beautiful statues, separated by two semi-columns , with an figurative frieze.

You'll be amazed at the beauty and silence of this location.

But let's quit talking about dead now.

We're heading right to the center of the path now and we'll arrive only a few steps from the entry point, at the most stunning building in the Ruins.

#002 The largest monument The Amphitheater. Amphitheater

It is believed that the Amphitheatre of Pompeii was buried during the eruption in 79 a.D. It is the oldest of the Roman age, and one of the best preserved in the world.

It was built in the 70s a.D. It was used to host spectacles of circus and also for fight between gladiators in addition to other parades and occasions.

You can witness it all through wall art and graffiti in the space.

The city of Pompeii there are numerous murals and graffiti illustrating these facts.

The Amphitheatre is located in the southern-east of Pompeii the suburbs of the city's past that in the time of Pompeii was not that crowded or was not so populated.

It was the perfect place to host large events like the sports or the events that were devoted to the residents. Furthermore, its construction attached to the town-wall made the construction much easier.

With the capacity of 20,000 people, it was the stage for major events as early as Roman times as well as in modern times.

Does it look small? Sure it is...if you compare it with modern stadiums like San Siro in Milan that can accommodate more than 80,000 spectators.

However, wait... You should be aware that Pompeii was home to around 20,000 people however the actual city of Milan is home to more or less 1,300,000 inhabitants. It's not difficult to determine out that the

Amphitheatre in Pompeii could accommodate 100percent of the population in Milan, whereas San Siro stadium can only accommodate San Siro stadium can host only 65% of Milan inhabitants.

As one of the biggest events held within it, I'd like to remind you that in the year 1971, the rock history was recorded in this area thanks to an iconic music event which I'm talking about as " Live at Pompeii".

Pink Floyd Pink Floyd recorded the first portion of their live movie concert without an audience.

In the space under the stairs, a photo gallery is now in place. It's dedicated to the show and you can view stunning photos from that historic concert , as well as the photos from the final one of David Gilmour in the Amphitheatre in 2016. Returning to Pompeii in the past 45 years. This one was performed live for the enjoyment of the fans who packed the Amphitheatre.

After visiting the gallery, you'll be shortly in the arena. Then walk to its center. Take a deep breath and close your eyes.

Are you able to hear the shouts of the crowd? Do you feel the excitement of the audience? Do you feel the power and determination of gladiators who fight to save themselves?

Chapter 2: Continue With The Big Palaestra

On the left edge to the left of Amphitheatre Square, directly in the front of the entrance to the Amphitheatre it is possible to enter in the Large Palaestra It is a massive magnificent and intriguing construction.

The building was constructed at the beginning of I century a.D. It was a place for the education of young Pompeiians. It appears that it was constructed in the will of Emperor Augusto following some changes in the policy for strengthening the Empire.

It's a vast green square that is surrounded by arcades. In the center is an enormous swimming pool that covers 800 square metres.

The structure was affected by the earthquake in 62 a.D. and was then destroyed when the volcano erupted in the eruption of 79 a.D.

Palestra Grande is famous for two reasons. Palestra Grande is famous for two reasons: within the area, many victims were found, escaping from the devastation of the volcano.

On the columns, you can see a variety of graffiti, written by writers of that time. One of them, perhaps the most famous is known as the Magic Square, the most oldest one to be discovered.

Are you able to figure out what is it and why it's crucial?

It's a weird word pun, a combination of five palindromes, which is five words you can read from the left and right side, as well as from the up verse as well as from the bottom verse.

It's famous becauseover the years scientists have tried to provide different interpretations of the phenomenon and have proposed theories that are connected to religion, politics and the esoteric.

The mysterious symbol has been seen in various times after this as well as in various parts of the globe.

After a reconstruction that lasted 7 years In 2015, the museum was opened for visitors. It now is home to the permanent exhibition of the research of Moregine.

It isn't permitted to walk into the open part of the Palaestra however, you are able to only stroll across the arcades on the lateral side.

The most popular selfies.

The rendition of the cover from the Beatles album "Abbey Road" modified using the pedestrian crossing in Pompeii is extremely famous.

#04 Let's accelerate and here we are in Via dell'Abbondanza

The visit to the Amphitheatre as well as it's Large Palaestra and the exhibitions described will take between 30 and 40 minutes.

Now it's time to proceed quickly along Via dell'Abbondanza.

One of the principal streets in Pompeii The main one, called Via dill'Abbondanza which is the one that connects Sarno Gate to the Forum.

The name was given due to an incorrect belief that the goddes are depicted in a low-relief carved into the rock of the fountain that is located close to the Forum. It's a fountain in white that depicts the eyes of a woman with a tunic, and a cornucopia.

It was mistaken for Goddess of Abundance However, that is the goddess Concordia Augusta.

The street is extremely crowded.

Similar to how it was, it's also one of the main attractions of the city, where we observe the main aspects of the day-to-day activities of Pompeii and the major public structures.

It was the avenue of commerce, brimming of restaurants and shops (pergulae).

There is, as other streets in Pompeii there is a large block of rock connecting these two walkways. These were the old crosswalks that let pedestrians cross the streets in the event that rainwater flooded the streets.

The space between rocks are big enough to allow for the movement of wheeled drays.

#05 Let's see Pompeii's domus. Pompeii

The patrician residence in Ancient Pompeii was referred to as Domus.

Let's look at its structure.

The entrance is an atrium, which was a huge area with a pool in the middle, with the intention collecting rainwater, also known as the impluvium. Bedrooms were referred to as cubicula, and they were oriented towards the atrium like the living rooms as well as the dining room.

Triclinium is famousbecause It was the location in which they dined and hosted guests. The name is derived of the 3 beds which the guests sat during banquets.

Through a corridor, you will arrive at the Peristyle, an arcade the center of which is an outdoor garden that is dotted featuring sculptures, painted edges and mosaics.

Domus, owned by wealthy people also had a small thermal site.

In this article, I'll talk about the 3 first domus will be on display on Via dell'Abbondanza. I'm hoping you'll get to see at least two of them.

They're all beautiful, however towards the close of this paragraph, I'll share my personal favorite.

The Praedia of Giulia Felice

It's among the most gorgeous and spacious domus in the city. which is defined as "villa urbana"(urban home) it is a keeper of the remains of an orchard as well as an enclosing garden.

It's 5.800 square meters and contains A thermal site as well as a tavern along with shops and apartments that are surrounded by a huge garden.

A wall art work has been discovered on the wall facing the front which indicates that these apartments generally rented. In real terms Giulia Felice, the proprietor Giulia Felice had an excellent business acumen and had created what we call B&B that included a spa that welcomed guests seeking wellbeing and sensorial relaxation.

It is also the finest part of the structure and has been reconstructed using the original plant life.

Laurel, ivy, and roses are a part of the fountain's design while vines make an arch on the oriental part in the gardens.

The area that the matrona lived in is reminiscent of the inside of a patrician villa, with beautiful paintings and statues that are that are on display in the Archaeological Museum of Naples.

In 2016, the work to restore the villa was completed and was opened to the public once more.

It's part of the itinerary " Pompei per tutti" It's a route that is accessible to all, and also for those with motor impairments.

House of Venus in the shell

In the opposite direction to the entrance, in the lower part of the peristyle is the window that appears to overlook the ocean. There's a beautiful artwork of Venus the goddess of love of Pompeii sitting in a shell, while waves swirl around her. There is a couple of cupids.

The painting was inspired by Esodo's story, " The born of Venus in the shell" in which it is said that Venus, the Venus goddess was born into the ocean's waves and was transported into Cyprus via Zephyr. When she arrived, the Ore took her to visit the other Gods.

Venus is naked. She wears only a diadem that is cut as Flavious age, a few anklets, and a gold bracelet. Venus has a hand fan. Near Venus she has her lover Mars which is painted on a side panel.

According to some researchers experts, it could be the roman version of that famous painting of Campaspe Alessandro Magno's love, drawn by Apelle, the most well-known artist of the time, Apelle.

It's a stunning and a tragic home at the same time constructed by a prominent family from the same time. It was damaged by the eruption of 62 a.D. explosion.

The restoration work began but the restoration was destroyed when the eruption occurred in the eruption of 79 a.D. which included the entire population.

It was not abandoned by fate even after excavation: during WWII, in 1943, it was struck by massive bombardments.

The lush garden and numerous paintings make this domus beautiful.

The House of Octavius Quartio

The house is located within Via dell'Abbondanza too.

According to historical records, it is the home of Loreius Tiburtinus. In fact, this is confirmed by the wall painting on the front.

It's a unique domus in particular because of the elements that are influenced by Egyptian culture, for example , the wall decoration and marble statues. The garden is lovely with a variety of plants as well as small pools that have water choreographies.

Here's the link to an amazing video in 3D graphic that shows how to reconstruct Octavius Quarto's home.

In the Regio II we complete this route before walking swiftly towards the Forum.

Oh, wait! ....I didn't inform you the domus that is my most favorite one.

Try to make a guess...

I'm sure you'd think it's the home that was the home of Giulia Felice...instead...

My favorite domus is the one that is the last, the house that was the home of Octavio Quartio.

And what's yours?

#06 Now let's look at the life of a productive man with Stephanus's Fullery of Stephanus

Prior to the eruption of Vesuvius the life of Pompeii was lively, it was a city with many people employed in productive tasks.

In this region of Campania the work of the laundryman is clearly visible. They were involved in cleaning, working and tingling the wool.

In Pompeii you can see the building known as Fullery which means laundry. It was which was owned by Stephanus. We have that the building's owner's name through the wall's inscription.

The Fullery could be compared to an actual modern-day industry: There was, in actual an refectory as well, in which workers could stay and eat during their working hours.

Fulleries were employed to wash the cloths following the process of filature and tessiture, as well as to simply wash the cloths.

Apart from the impluvium which is where the bulk of the water needed for wash was taken there are 5 additional pools that are linked to the other as well as 5 additional pools that are used to wash or to tint the tissues.

Pestles "kneaded" clothes using soda and water (Pompeiians didn't know the soap that was used for cleaning in Gallia) or even with human urine.

The public restrooms were that were dedicated to the collection of urine, a process known as vespasiani in honor of the emperor who enacted the decree.

After treatment, the cloths were cleaned with chalk or with umbric powder after which they were pounded and carded.

White or colored ones were treated using sulfur in order to be polished.

The final stage was pressing, which was done with stone presses.

This fullery also had the top floor, which had an outdoor space where they could hang laundry.

In the office at the other side of the house, they discovered an skeleton containing gold and silver coins with the sum of 10.000 euros.

You're probably exhausted after your visit to the Fullery and would like to refresh. On your left you'll find the structure known as "The House of the Eagle" in which you will have access to public toilets , while you're there, you can take a look from the air of the archaeological area.

#07 is among the most ancient of the Roman world: Stabian Baths

We arrived at the second half of our trip, exactly at the intersection of Main Decuman and Stabiana Street. This is where you'll find The Stabian Baths (the baths) located in a public space 3.500 sqm in size.

There are times when it gets crowded. I believe you'll need to wait for a couple of minutes before you can gain access to.

At the entry point, you'll be taken to a vast area that was used for gymnasium.

The thermal baths in the Roman period were divided into segments, and one was dedicated to males and the other was for women.

To the left, going via an arcade come to the male area, located in the " Apodyterioum" prior to (it was a kind alter room) before moving on to the frigidarium, which was a bath that was filled with cold water. Then you'll get to the tepidarium where the bathers took a bath in warm water. They then went finally, to the calidarium, hot bathing.

The heating system in the roman baths was in the forefront.

There was a tube plant in the walls as well as the floor was constructed with the double stratum system which let the flow of hot air that came out of the furnaces.

Returning to the garden to the left of the entry point, you'll find the pool.

Near the far end at the end of the garden, along the northwest you'll find access to the female's area which is smaller and less decorated in comparison to the other.

Here's another URL of a video-clip in which you can watch how baths were created.

If you want to continue on your way, you can leave the baths through the entrance that is facing Lupanar Street where you'll enjoy the experience of visiting some of the more stunning locations in the city.

#08 The oldest brothel The Lupanar

Roman people were fond of fun in public events, liberty and play.

Lupanar are unique locations, they were districts of the city that were dedicated to sexual pleasure " Red-light Quarters".

In antiquated Pompeii there were brothels: There were 25 brothels were found throughout the city.

Lupanar is among the most popular tourist destinations and you'll most likely need to wait in line to get there.

If you're running out of time and are traveling with your family, I would suggest that you skip this step, and it's surely not the best choice for children.

The tale of the lupanar is told through the murals on the walls.

In reality there are a variety of representations of erotic positions. It's similar to an old kamasutra.

The building is composed of two levels, one of which was occupied by slaves as well as the owner.

The lower level was divided into five rooms equipped with beds made of stone very small and dark, so that Pompeiians could satisfy any sexual desire of slaves.

It is important to look at the graffiti that lists the names of customers or prostitutes as well as remarks on sexual positions and occasionally, advice on the sexual illnesses that are circulating.

It's obvious that during the Roman era, prostitution wasn't legal, but they were heavily involved in promoting and searching activities that were aimed at satisfying sexual desires of the people and so throughout the streets, as they brought to brothels you can observe, expertly built in the wall or the floor, depictions of phallus, indicating the proper direction to get there.

More information is available on this short video "erotic arts from Pompeii".

Chapter 3: The Forum Of Pompeii, The Area In Which Everything Takes Place

From the Lupanar return on Via dell'Abbondanza and quickly reach the final stretch of the road, and arrive at the Forum. There you will be able to take some time to relax.

I would suggest taking a an unplanned break during which you can eat something that you brought with you , or take some great photos using the classic "postcard" image of Mount Vesuvius on the background.

The Forum is a further essential part of a city in Rome that is a central square the place where people get together to conduct business, vote and debates about the state of affairs, prays and purchases.

It's the true heart of the community.

It's located at the intersection of the principal street of the capital city. The first entry point is one of the most terrifying and enormous Vesuvius just behind the Temple of Jupiter and on the opposite side is the sea. The second is to

Nocera in one direction and then to Naples on the other .

Let's sit in the middle of the Forum of Pompeii, looking at the Temple of Jupiter Let's think about the incredibleness of this location. be prior to the time that Vesuvius beautiful, but brutal awakened and destroyed the city.

There are many important public buildings like temples and the Basilica and other structures that are dedicated to the city's administration and other buildings destined for the market.

In the middle of the square, and close to this, the massive works by Igor Mitoraj are exposed.

Don't miss out on the photo featuring the sculpture of the Centaur and is an absolute hit with tourists.

The bronze work is set in a square and stretches out with its spear.

The Forum of the Ruins of Pompeii is without doubt the best preserved Forum in all of the other Italian antiquated cities.

A curiosity to learn about

When Vesuvius was exploding, there was an election in the process. You can see today on the city's walls that the campaign's sponsors were dedicated to the election campaign They suggested voting on one candidate in lieu of another...but the election day was never a reality.

#10 The Basilica isn't a church , but an administrative tribunal

The Forum as well to demand justice. Today, we still use the term "Foro" to signify the court ("for any future disputes" it's stated in the contracts we make, "it will be under the jurisdiction that of Forum in ...").

Justice was administered in the Basilica which was located on the lower part of the square, right in the front of the Comitium.

The name of the building and the interior design of the room, which includes columns that run through the aisles are a nod to our contemporary churches.

For Pompeiians and all cities in the Roman Empire there was a difference the basilica actually served as the tribunal, which was a covered area where the judge handed down his decision after hearing the lawyers.

The judge was seated on the cathedra, at the center aisle's bottom and, in our churches - is the bishop.

11. Final step Final step: The Temples Temples

What is the time that has passed?

We surpassed our 2 hours. Are you exhausted?

Let's get going... it's just an effort to get it done We're at the final step.

Pompeii is an Latin city. Its urban structure is also tied to religion, particularly the old pagan one deeply embedded in the Empire as a whole.

On the slopes of Vesuvius sacred rituals can't be missed. The temples are the best of them.

In the final moments of your trip to the temple, spend a few minutes within one of these beautiful temples.

It is the Temple of Apollo, situated on the left of the Forum.

Affirmed to Apollo The temple is believed to be built in the seventh century b.C. It is awash with altars, it's a structure that may be in use until the Samnite period.

This is the most important sacred site of The city of the same name, and as numerous murals and cuts exhibit, or statues and other artifacts.

It is the Temple of Jupiter, on the north end of the Forum.

It's as old in its cult divinity, but it's also a crucial element of Roman culture. In Pompeii this Temple can't be left out. It was constructed, actually, in the year 250 b.C.

It was progressively growing and became more attractive, distinctive. It's among the most unique places dedicated to Jupiter.

It is the Temple of Venus, out of the area of Forum situated along Marina Street.

There is a temple in every roman city and is which is dedicated to Goddess. It's in Pompeii from.

It's located in the highest point of the valley. It offers a stunning view with a view of its view of the Gulf of Naples. The story behind it is unique and intricate.

We're almost there ....or but maybe not?

If you follow Marina Street, after a steep slope of pebbles will lead you the Marina Gate.

If you've finished your time devoted to visiting the Ruins then you can use this exit to leave.

I'm certain you've followed all the steps I recommended and are now exhausted.

Do you have some spare time?

Here is a brief list of other steps you could add to your journey through the most famous archeological site in the world.

* Antiquarium

* Theatres

* Macellum

"House of the Vettii

* House of the Small Fountain

* Villa of the Mysteries

Your short but intense trip to the remains of Pompeii is over.

The only thing you need to do is buy something to remember. An ebook, memento or a gadget you can present to family or friends You can discover it as you exit at Marina Gate

At the exit, you will be able to get a train to go back to Naples...it is very simple.

Chapter 4: What Should You Do After Pompeii When You Have A Half Day Off

Hello, and welcome back.

Have you completed your journey through the past?

Have you had the chance to explore the intriguing and mysterious world that lies within Pompeii's walls? Pompeii?

I'm sure , even with you have only a few hours the places you visited have emitted to you a lot of memories and you're willing to share these stories with passion to your acquaintances.

Hello... If you share a photo to Facebook or Instagram don't be forgetting to tag me using the hashtag is #Pompeiitaly.

Everyday I post on Instagram the best pictures of the tourists who visited Pompeii and the number of followers on the account @Pompeiitaly is growing each day... We have more than 20.000 people, but I am always working hard to bring the beauty of my area to a greater number of people.

My goal is to establish the Community of Pompeii Ambassadors, Join us!

The journey continues. in the future, I'll offer a suggestions on how to plan your remaining time.

Perfect joint

Before I wrote this guide, I conducted a poll among my readers.

Of the numerous questions I asked to comprehend the most beneficial information I could provide to you I also asked:

"How many hours will you devote to your trip to Pompeii".

The most frequently asked question was:

"1 day".

It didn't seem to me like something that was odd.

Pompeii has always been way too short a stage in the plans of travellers, but as I frequently reiterate, it deserves an in-depth excursion.

As I said I'm a traveler as well and, as you, I plan my travels to be at the top of the hill in my destination. I try to join as many destinations as I can to ensure that I ensure that I don't miss anything and, at times, I'm exhausted, to the point that I'll need a break! This is why I relate to you.

Be assured don't worry, in this part of the book I'll provide you some intriguing ideas on the most intriguing things to do around here the time you've planned, for the majority of visitors to Pompeii only one day here.

I'll give you three paths that cover a variety of areas of interest.

The options I'll present will allow you to seamlessly join in the excursion to this Archaeological site.

You can select between them based on your preference or in accordance with the schedule that is set by the Ruins.

If you don't find here the suggestions you were looking for don't hesitate to send me an email at travelguide@pompeiitaly.org

As the subject of the letter, compose "Maria I'd like to have more ideas regarding Pompeii".

This will help me realize that you're a follower of this book and I'll respond within 24 hours.

3 VISITS IN CONJUNCTION to POMPEII

* The Shrine of Pompeii

For those who love art and religion.

The time required for the visit Time required for the visit: 2 hours

Don't forget to visit the belvedere on to the Bell Tower of the shrine

* Oplontis

For lovers of archeology and historical research.

The duration of the visit Time required for the visit: 2 hours

Don't forget your chance to admire the splendor of this gardens and the vivid colors of the paintings

* Sorrento

For lovers of the sea and boroughs

Time required to visit the site The visit should last between 2-4 hours.

Shopping along the main street, Corso, is a essential, as are the views from the Communal Villa

SHRINE OF POMPEII

Not just archaeology, but also Pompeii

I recommend you to go to it prior to beginning the excursion to the Ruins or perhaps in the afternoon , to finish the day. The time required for the tour 2 hours

You've followed the travel route I recommended to you. You reached Pompeii with the Circumvesuviana train, which departed to the stops Pompei Santuario?

The first part of the city is the tour of the impressive Shrine that is Our Lady of the Rosary of Pompeii.

It's located 100 meters. away from the train station, and it's easy to access it.

After you have visited the Shrine and bell tower, you are able to go to the archeological site.

If you began your tour of the Ruins by following the opposite of my advice and you began at Porta Marina and arrived at Porta Anfiteatro. From there, you can get to in just 7-8 minutes walking through the city's centre including the massive and often busy Piazza Bartolo Longo, the area facing the shrine.

It's not a bad idea to go to the Shrine It's important devote around two hours.

There's no ticket to enter So it's totally cost-free.

After you have finished visiting the church, you are able to enjoy stunning city views from the tower's bell of Pompeii.

More than 80m in elevation, it permits you to admire the stunning urban landscape, the breathtaking view of a magnificent landscape.

It's the ideal spot to take advantage of as a backdrop for great photos of your trip here!

Do not worry, you do not need to climb the nearly 300 steps of the stairwell There's a lift which will take you up.

Let's continue and learn more on one of the most significant catholic centres in Italy.

The Shrine of Our Lady of the Rosary of Pompeii...a little bit of the past

The Shrine Our Lady of the Rosary of Pompeii was established in the latter part of the 1800s close to The Archaeological area of the old Roman city.

Its story is tied to the story of a lawyer Bartolo Longo who was blessed in the year 1980 in 1980 by Pope John Paul II.

The construction began in 1876 at the 8th of May, which saw the placing on the foundation stone. it was constructed thanks to the generous donations that came from the faithful of all over the world. The construction was completed on the 7th day of May, 1891 following the consecration performed by Cardinal Raffaele Monaco. La Valletta.

The Basilica was designed through Antonio Cua, professor at the University of Naples, who created and directed the construction until 1889 when it was the time that architect Giovanni Rispoli alternated him.

The shrine was originally just the one Latin cross nave, with an dome, apse and side chapels. Its area was 442 sq m.

In the end, when considering the huge numbers of pilgrims and faithful it was decided to expand the area. The project was completed in the years 1934-1939 and transformed it to Basilica to its current size that included 3 Latin cross naves, and an area of 2.000 square meters that could accommodate 6.000 people.

The Shrine, right from the time of its construction until today it has survived many hardships like the eruption of Vesuvius in 1944, and the invading of Nazi troops , who threatened to take it down.

The façade of the Shrine

When you arrive at the area behind the building you'll be able to see the impressive façade dedicated to peace for all.

The construction started in 1894. It was officially opened on the 5th May 1901.

It was planned and conceived by architect Rispoli.

The building was built by the efforts of devotees from around the globe who were part of the plebiscite that was arranged to the founding father of Pompeii as illustrated by the numerous documents of signatures that are preserved in the archives of the past "Bartolo Longo".

The façade of the shrine in Pompeii is made from Travertine blocks sourced out of Monte Tifate, in Sant'Angelo in Formis the same material used in the construction of the Tower of the Church of Santa Chiara in Naples as well as in the Royal Palace of Caserta.

It's like a church, and is composed of two floors.

On the lower level which is constructed in the ionic order there are three arcades, and further ahead there's a stairwell that connects the porch with the square.

In the lower portion of the first order, there's an unfinished base that has four columns of pink granite from the Gravellona region On both sides, you'll find four lesenes.

Between the lower and the upper one, an elongated ledge of pink granite protrudes. It shows the inscribed

"VIRGINI SS. ROSARII DICATUM".

The second floor, which is in Corinthian order, is based on the same layout as the floor before it.

In the center is Pope's lodge. It's decorated with two tiny pilasters that show the emblems of the founders.

On the opposite side of the large window that faces over the lodge is a pair of columns constructed from Red granite from Finland and two capitals made from Carrara marble.

On the fronton that encloses the central area, there's the arms of the pope Leone XIII who declared the Shrine "Pontifical Sanctuary".

On its two sides , there are two windows that are smaller.

The three windows illuminate the large hall which houses the Historical Archives "Bartolo Longo".

A cornice of grey granite separates the second section from the attic by an eaves-style balustrade. On it is an sculptural work of art depicting in the Virgin of the Rosary with the Holy Child at 3,25 meters tall statue that was sculpted by the sculpture artist Gaetano Chiaromonte. He created it using a single piece of Carrara marble with a weight at 180 quintals.

At the bottom, which functions as a pedestal, inscriptions PAX and MCM, which refer to the year of its inception are prominently displayed.

The balustrade is enhanced by a clock that can be used as a dialogic one as well as a meridian one as well, which is arranged with two decorative round, to match the windows on either side.

The three entry doors have been decorated in white marble. on the center one, there's an arch and below this there are two cherubim adorned with the iris and roses, as well as the inscribed BASILICA PONTIFICIA.

The dome's central part is stunning and is adorned with eight pairs of granite columns of Corinthian order, as well as eight windows decorated with vibrant windows and ornaments.

The upper portion is covered with double ribs, and at its bottom is an travertine column of granite that form the cusp's base, which is also covered with copper and a cross at the top. The dome is flanked by four domes smaller than it, made from the same structural components.

The lower part of the walls that surround Basilica Basilica is covered by an edging of red granite from Baveno that covers the entire structure.

On the plinth is a the travertine of Tivoli that supports 20 columns constructed of granite. On the apex of each column is a capital with bas-reliefs as well as angel heads that are supporting the cornice. Above that is an baluster of travertine.

The Apses of the side altars are extremely relevant.

Particularly on the East side and on the vertical side of the dome is the apse of the church that is the chapel of Saint Joseph, which ends with a pediment, on which is inscribed the arms and coat of Pope Pius XI.

On the opposite side is the risalit which is similar to the apse in the chapel that is St Michael, very similar to the other, but concluding with a pediment which is inscribed the arms and coat of arms Bartolo Longo.

"The Picture of the Virgin

It's time to go into this Shrine in order to allow the spirituality and sanctity this place fill the entire space.

Be quiet and careful as you travel along the side naves. be sure to glance at the frescoes as well as at the statues, take to the right and look up at at the magnificent frescoes in Central nave.

In front of you is the massive and solemn Main Altar, where you can take in the view of one the most powerful symbol of devotion and faith The painting depicting Jesus Christ as the Virgin in Pompeii.

It is well-known all across the globe as a tourist destination, it draws millions of visitors each year.

The artist who painted the Virgin of the Rosary is not identified. I will tell you how the painting's arrival here in Pompeii because of Bartolo Longo towards the end of the 1800s.

The image is 120cm high and 100cm wide. It depicts the Virgin sitting on a throne, with the Holy Child resting on her legs.

Saint Domenico receives from the hand of Jesus the Rosary and Saint Caterina from Siena receives it from the left side from the Virgin. Both saints are at the feet of the Virgin.

The background of the Picture of the Virgin is closely related to the story of the blessed Bartolo Longo, who tried to spread practices of praying the Rosary traveled to Naples for the purpose of purchase an artwork he had seen only a short time prior in an art shop.

In the name of God, he met Padre Redente the confessor to him, who advised him to visit the Conservatory of the Rosary of Portamedina in his honor and also to request to Suor Maria Concetta De Litala to present a painting that he had gifted her 10 years earlier.

Bartolo followed his advice, however, he was shocked by the way his sister presented the painting, the canvas was worn and tarnished that was missing parts of color and a representation of the Madonna carrying the crown to Santa Rosa in place of Santa Caterina from Siena in the Dominican tradition.

Bartolo was on the verge of deciding to reject the offer However, in the end , he decided to decline the gift in order to satisfy the sake by the Nun.

Its image of Madonna was transported to Pompeii and reached the Parish of the SS. Salvatore in the 13th November 1875. The image was wrapped in a cloth and was carried in a cart driven by Angelo Tortora. This cart served for transporting manure.

People who were present at the time that the painting was unveiled shared the same reactions as Bartolo Longo. They remained in shock. Also, there was the old church Cirillo.

Thus the decision to move on with the restoration photograph was taken even if it was only partially due to the fear that it might be damaged.

The initial part of the restoration was created by Guglielmo Galella an artist who gained a lot of attention in Pompeii due to his paintings of frescoes from the ruin.

As time passed the old canvas worsened and was then restored time by Neapolitan artist Federico Maldarelli, who had also taken care to alter the image depicted in Saint Rosa to Saint Caterina in Siena.

Following that, Francesco Chiariello, another Neapolitan artist, repainted the canvas by stretching it over a just a few centimeters. After that, the real restoration was done by Maldarelli.

Another restoration was completed during the year 1965 by the Pontifical Institute of the Order of Our Lady of Mount Olivet in Rome.

The restoration enabled them to find the original colors of the canvas which showed the talents of an artist from that school, Luca Giordano (17 th century) and removed nearly all gemstones in order to prevent any further damage or punctures to the canvas.

The image of the Virgin was in view for the veneration of faithful for a few days in the Basilica of Saint Peter and on the 23rd day of April, it was celebrated with the blessing of Pope Paul VI.

Return of The Picture of the Madonna of Pompeii was celebrated with solemnity by a procession of faithful and ecclesiastics that expanded as it passed through cities, on its route between Rome to Pompeii which was where the trip was concluded with a grand finale.

A final restoration was enacted at the time of The pope Benedict XVI. Restoration specialists from the Vatican Museum started to work on the canvas to remove the damage caused by the silver and gold clips that were hung to the canvas as a gift to the Virgin Mary.

The pilgrims and pilgrims all around world gather to the shrine to offer the Rosary every day on the 8th of May, and also at the beginning of each Sunday in October. They proclaim"supplica "Supplica"(a request to Mary, written by the saintly Bartolo Longo) and ask God to bring peace to all the world.

Another significant celebration, that is extremely heartfelt for those who believe in The Virgin of the Rosary is the kissing of the image that is created each year to commemorate the anniversary of the first entry into Pompeii.

On this day each year an apex of the artwork is completed and is hung on the front of the presbytery to allow the faithful to walk up and worship and praise the Virgin Mary with kisses.

Find out the former voto

In the course of the year, billions of people go to The Shrine, Temple of the Spirit it is a place for reconciliation and conversion, prayers and mercy, a secure refuge for those who believe in the faith.

Even if you're not Catholic A visit to Pompeii's Shrine of Pompeii can gift the visitor with great feelings due to its majestic architecture as well as its exquisite and beautiful decorations.

After you have left the Basilica, I recommend you to go to in the chapel of the ex-voto to devotional that is which is dedicated to Our Virgin of the Rosary.

The ex-voto are the most tangible testimony that the faithful, due to prayer and the intercession of Mary, the Virgin Mary received blessings that helped them overcome difficult times and deep suffering.

The moment you enter this space and walk through the corridors to the walls of which the various ex-voto have been exposed, can bring you to such a profound feeling that you feel the happiness and gratitude of those who, through their talents wish to display the mercy that is Our Lady.

Ex-voto is a term used to describe objects, photos or paintings, as well as texts that are offered to the Virgin in gratitude for grace received.

They aren't just an act of faith they are also a permanent memories of a deep love for the Holy Virgin Mary as well as Bartolo Longo who listens to prayers and pray to God.

In actuality, offering an extra vote to Our Lady of Pompeii is just the final act in an extensive and complicated process that starts with a prayer for divine intervention, then the execution of the request followed by the visit towards The Blessed Virgin Picture to let go of the obligation of voting and culminates in the presentation of the gift that makes an eternal mark the grace that was received.

Do not miss the spectacular panorama from the Bell tower.

You can extend your visit at the Shrine by visiting the Museum in which a variety of items from all over the globe are kept however, if you are short on time, I would suggest that you climb to the highest point to the Bell tower.

The ticket is priced at 2 euros. You can purchase it from the store of religious gifts located next to the Church.

The Bell tower in spring and summer months all day long, between 8.00 until 20.00 On Sundays and Saturdays, it's open until 22:00.

In winter , and until the 30th of April, the closing time is set at 18,00 on the week and 19,00 on Sunday and on Saturday.

The last amount that can be earned is 15 minutes prior to end of the day.

The sole access to this tower Bell tower is through a relaxing lift that will lead visitors to the balcony from where you can take an hour or two and take in the views.

One of the tallest towers in Italy

A stunning view from that of the Pompeii Valley, the archaeological site, and The Gulf of Naples.

The top of the Bell tower in Pompeii is 82m, making it one of the tallest in Italy when we take into account bell towers over 90 meters in height (in Italy there are 15 in total).

Due to some difficulties due to the consistency of the soil , it was constructed on a foundation constructed of bars of concrete with armored joints that were pushed to a depth of 20 meters.

The design was created with the help of Aristide And Pio Leonori, the building was inaugurated by an solemn ceremony on May 24th, 1925 before the presence of Bartolo Longo, following 13 years of laying the initial stone.

Its structure is split into three components:

An exterior area covered in gray and white marble. The inside is brick part as well as an inside one constructed of iron to support the 360 steps of a staircase along with an elevator.

It's constructed in Corinthian style and is distinguished by five overlaid architectural orders, the last of which is an outdoor terrace with a balustrade that allows you to view an awe-inspiring belvedere in the bell tower in Pompeii that is located in the Valley of Naples, the Excavations as well as the Gulf of Naples.

The first is the one at the front of the tower. This is achieved through a massive bronze door with high relief, depicting what appears to be the appearance of the holy heart to Saint. Margaret Mary Alacoque.

The pedestals from the 3rd order, four bronze angels are set.

A system of electricity makes the eight bells operate. The bells are constructed of different dimensions , which means they sound different.

The bigger bell is two-meter diameter, and hangs 50 quintals.

In a niche on the fourth floor, there's an image of the Sacred Heart of Jesus, 5 meters tall with the total weight of around 180 quintals. The statue is composed from Carrara marble.

Its Bell Tower is decorated by bronze dome, over which is a cross of bronze and copper. It's 7 meters tall, and it's lit up at night , so it's visible from a distance of several kilometers.

The views of this Bell tower is truly breathtaking and the entire city is right at our feet. If you look further ahead and you'll be able to see The Ruins of Pompeii as a relic to the magnificence of this city.

But the feelings aren't gone because at the horizon, it is possible to observe an area called the Gulf of Naples and on the right is splendor the Vesuvius.

Chapter 5: Oplontis And The Villa Of Poppea

I would suggest that you visit it prior to beginning the tour of the Ruins or perhaps later in the afternoon to end the day. The duration of the tour 2 hours

For you to continue your journey through the realm of Roman archeology and the past, I'd like to recommend you a treasure that's not so well-known to the large tourism influx in these regions the archeological site of Oplontis which is an off-the-beaten-path to Pompeii but is actually quite accessible.

To get to Oplontis you need to get to at least one station connecting Pompeii with the city of Rome, and then go to Torre Annunziata, the current name of the old Oplontis. It is only two minutes away.

The nearest station to the Oplontis excavations lies on the Circumvesuviana train line.

If you're driving from Pompeii then follow the A3 or E45 motorway to Naples and leave at Torre Annunziata Sud.

If you have a some hours to spend in the early morning hours, focus on the major tourist attractions of Pompeii and later in the afternoon, go to Oplontis Be aware that last admission will be around 18.00 from April through October, and at 15.30 in winter.

Two hours for this trip is enough, and although trains are not long it is important to think about an overall time of 3 hours for the journey.

If you are planning to combine the visit of Pompeii along with the excavations at Oplontis I would suggest that you purchase the ticket for the whole trip for the price of 14 euros. For children it's free.

As a result, you'll be able to gain access to 3 archeological sites for three days

(Oplontis, Boscoreale, Pompeii).

Tickets are available to purchase on the internet, for both archaeological sites, through the Ticketone official website. This way, you won't have to wait in line at the ticket booth. Make sure to print it out and bring the ticket with the ticket you purchase.

The Oplontis Discovery

Oplontis is located near and is located near the Ruins of Pompeii The name of the town is the origin of the present Torre Annunziata, and its archaeological excavations are situated in the middle of the city's new construction.

It was also overrun by the Vesuvius lava in the eruption of 79 a.D. volcanic eruption.

The first signs of its existence first began to appear in early Middle Ages.

Oplontis was classified as a suburb of Pompeii and was a place of choice to rest.

What can you expect to see in this tiny, ancient city, which was made by the remains from Mount Vesuvius and that has remained remaining intact?

In the archaeological finds we can find: Villa of Poppea; an old-fashioned villa that is believed to be the property of L. Crassius Tertius, where bodies that were uncovered and involved in everyday activities were found and also coins in silver and gold too; an spa structure that was part of today's Terme Nunziante.

The only site that is accessible can be found in the Villa of Poppea, come and visit it.

Villa of Poppea

It was constructed around the 1st century b.C. It is the only monument that can be visited of the Oplontis ancient.

UNESCO World Heritage Site, it's a private residence and is part of imperial history. The architecture as well as the frescoes have a royal look and blend well to the geometries formed by columns and walls.

The western portion is accessible but is yet to be completely submerged in the east, whereas the western part is almost fully accessible.

At the time of the eruption, it was in the process of being restored, but it was empty, possibly it was damaged due to the numerous earthquakes that struck the area during the time.

It appears to be belonging to Poppea Sabina, who was the Second wife of Emperor Nerone.

The splendor of this Villa in addition to its extraordinary size and structure, could be due to the amazing parietal frescoes that are nearly completely preserved.

You should take a look at it. Cassata di Oplontis, a cake that is painted in the wall of the triclinium, which recalls the Sicilian cassata. It is likely made of marzipan and fruits; The famous basket, with figs and the columns of gold and the amorini, the depiction of the seasons and many more.

A DRIVE TO SORRENTO

The name is known all around the world.

I would suggest that you go to it at the end of the day or evening at the close to the day.

The time required for the visit The visit should last between 2-4 hours.

It's not just about history, but also nature, sea , and beautiful things.

The Gulf of Naples there are plenty of dream locations: Capri rests laid down like queen on the Tyrrhenian sea, along with Ischia Procida and Ischia Procida.

There is also Sorrento.

Yes, I'll take your to the Sorrento Peninsula, also celebrated by Luciano Pavarotti with the song "Torna a Surriento" with a unique rendition.

After a full day in Pompeii and Sorrento, a visit to Sorrento could be the perfect final icing before getting back home to conclude your time in these lands of sunshine.

To get to Sorrento you can take the Circumvesuviana train once more, but this time the line is Naples-Sorrento.

You can get the train from Pompeii via Pompei Scavi station right at the end of the archeological site.

If you follow my route, you'll find yourself going to the Excavations in Porta Marina and a few metres away is the station which will get you to Sorrento in just 30 minutes.

Are you in the area in a vehicle?

Follow the SS 145, the entrance is approximately 2 km from the site of archeological excavations and it is well-marked on the way.

By walking along the coast road, you will be able to enjoy stunning panoramas of the Sorrento peninsula. You'll reach your destination within 40 minutes .

Be aware that during the summer months, it can be a busy road , and the travel time could be longer.

Make sure you are aware of the traffic conditions before you leave for your journey.

It is not recommended to travel by car to Sorrento on a Sunday during the summer.

You can also look into hydrofoils on the sea. Starting from Naples Central Station, go to Molo Beverello and embark on one of the boats to Sorrento.

It's a fantastic adventure, but you may not be able schedule it if you are short on time.

What should you see in Sorrento

Sorrento was constructed on top of a ridge made of tuff. It is famous throughout the world because of its orange.

It's among the most adored destinations for visitors for its stunning landscapes that connect mountains and sea.

An authentic place to find spirit and inspiration for artists and writers.

It's believed to be linked to Capri through the shoreline that is Punta Campanella.

A lot of students are trying to prove this concept.

As seen from afar, Island Azzurra as well as Sorrento appear to be attempting to kiss.

The best route to explore the city could start with Piazza Tasso, the heart of the historical center and dedicated to the poet of the time. Jerusalem delivered.

From the point of arrival, you'll reach it in only a couple of minutes.

From here, you can go on to Corso Italia, a long shopping street.

Alongside the big bookshops, can find many boutiques devoted to food, crafts, and Ice-creams.

On one side that form Piazza Tasso, take a look at the Correale Museum of Terranova.

It houses artworks and paintings from an extended period of time from the 16th century until the late 19th century.

There is an opportunity to view Italian and porcelain from other countries, as well as watches and archaeological finds that date back to the beginning of the city.

Nearby to Piazza Tasso you can also go at the Lignea Tarsia Museum, inside the Pomarici Santomasi palace.

The building was constructed during the 1800s. It was it was restored in 1999.

Take note of its furniture and wooden items built with this technique. Sorrentino Inlay technique.

This crafty practice is an integral part of this area. It was established during the fifteenth century by Benedictine monks who lived in the church in the convent of S. Agrippino.

Through the streets narrow that wind through the town's old quarters,, you ought to stop and purchase an inlaid wooden piece. For instance, a carillon. It is a great idea for a unique gift an original piece.

In the same area, there is no way to overlook the Communal Villa and you'll be able to take in stunning views.

Your eyes will be lost in the blue of the sky and sea with only your eyes being able to see the "nearly drowned" designs of the close islands.

The monuments you should not ignore is The church that was built by Saint Francesco d'Assisi, which has an impressive cloister dating to the 18th century, as well as The church dedicated to St. Antonio, patron of the city.

In the church is an old nativity scene that dates to the year 1700.

Have you ever heard that celebrations of St. Anthony fell on the 14th of February?

Right, on Valentine's Day? Sorrento is awash with bright colors, lights and common sweets that are displayed along some of the streets.

Another thing to remember, while strolling around Corso Italia, do not overlook the adjacent San Cesareo lane.

These small streets are packed with hundreds of touristswho are attracted by the usual shops of liquor and leather items.

A dip in the sea

Sorrento is home to a wide range of beaches that are suitable for everyone Many of them have parking facilities.

The most stunning beaches in Marina Grande is the ancient seaside town. It's volcanic and has two hotels as well as a free zone where there's no fee to enter.

You'll be amazed by the numerous colorful houses and boats.

At times, you'll see fishermen who are trying to clean the fishing nets, or even gozzi.

Have you ever thought about the fact that throughout around the globe, Gozzi of Sorrento are synonymous with longevity and security?

These are small boats that have the shape of a tapered, and the length of a sail of 6-12 meters.

There's the beach of Marina Piccola, which can be reached from the center of Sorrento via the steps that have been built in the rocks.

If you do, you have the option of a private beach or a free one.

Small tip: Stop here for a taste of a delicious fish dish at one of the many restaurants within the zone.

These restaurants are surrounded by a beautiful ocean view.

Are you in search of an intimate experience?

This is the best answer for your needs!

It is the Cove of Mitigliano

The beach stands out from other beaches due to its pebbles and especially the crystal-clear waters. If you also enjoy trekking, it's the best option.

It is situated on shores in Massa Lubrense, situated in an inlet that is surrounded by olive groves and the Mediterranean area.

When you bathe or lie in the sun, you can be able to enjoy the view from the island Capri. To get to the beach, you'll need to follow the trail from Termini and follow the Via Campanella descent to the junction with Via Mitigliano.

If you're a diving lover, you should not ignore the stunning seaside beauty of the beachfront of Punta Campanella with gorgonias of every kind as well as tuna fish and rudderfishes.

In the depths you'll discover the yellow-colored sponge rug which is home to a multitude of small organisms that are waiting to be discovered.

Our trip has ended, you need to decide and get ready for an unforgettable journey.

Before you leave, check on the next pages the most important information that will make your trip truly memorable.

Chapter 6: The Inside Approach To The East

The second tour takes you deeper in the city. There are times when you walk to the south of the Street of Abundance, sometimes you'll walk to the north of it. The tour will eventually take you to the Forum through several of the town's public buildings , and other places as well.

For you to help you find your way with respect to the place you'll be This map will help you find your way around of the six places on the tour (Locations 12 through 17 starting from the 11th location of the first tour).

If you're able to do only half the tour due to the time limitations, then concentrate on the locations 15 and 16 specifically (simply because they're so different from what you've previously experienced) Although it would be disappointing in the event that you did not take in the location 12 (the House of Menander) Also, be aware the fact that Location 16 may not be suitable for everyone (being an establishment that is a brothel). There is a toilet at Location 15.

Place 12: The House of Menander (1.10.4)

The house is referred to by the name of House of Menander because one of the frescoes painted inside the residence depicts Menander, the well-known Greek writer Menander. There is no evidence that Menander lived in the house, but the lives of those who lived here end here with the eruption of Vesuvius. The remains of about thirteen people were discovered in the home. A few of the bones have been put on display inside the house within one of the rooms in the back located next to the dining room that is in the main.

Skeletons within the House of Menander

Although we do not identify the proprietor but we do recognize that the man was incredibly wealthy. Two factors suggest the affluence of the family members who resided at this residence: the home in itself, and what was located in the home. The first is that the house is a reflection of the lavishness of the family. This house is one of its largest ones in Pompeii. In the last 30 years of Pompeii's existence, the property began to take over the surrounding properties. The owner bought a part of the properties around it which he then accumulated to create an extremely luxurious homes in Pompeii. It is among the few homes in Pompeii that had slaves with their own quarters and luxurious quarters too. It was also among the houses that had its own bathing facility. It was also among the few houses to have its own stable and coach area.

(There are four primary components to the entire complex. (1) The original house at the center, (2) the central gardens and the colonnade peristyle that grew out of the house's original dimensions, (3) the further expansion of the slave quarters on the east side, and stables on the southeastern end as well as (4) an expansion in the kitchen and bath areas on the west side. A large portion of the western and eastern sides of the house remain closed to the public at present Unfortunately.)

What was also discovered in the house indicates lavishness. Before the eruption, a person inside the residence hid the bulk of silver dining ware within the bathing area in the house. This artifact is an uncommon find in Pompeii's homes. A collection of stunning jewelry was also found within the residence. A ring bearing the name "Quintus Poppaeus Eros" was discovered, which has led to some scholars that the family was connected to Poppaea Sabina who was a very attractive woman who was the mistress and later second wife of Emperor Nero. (We have other proof that the lineage of the family was linked to Pompeii Also, see below for Location 39, the House of the Golden Cupids.)

This suggests that the person who lived in the residence was prosperous as well as (therefore) powerful. It's no wonder that two stone benches were erected at in front of the home. They were intended for customers of the householder to relax on as they waited for access into the home so that they could see their patron of influence (as you'll recall from the premises of Julia Felix's). The clients would gather each morning to wait until their turn to be able to meet their patron possibly even before the initial sun's rays. They sought help and assistance from the householder and in return, were expected to take every chance to praise his work and boost his status with the local population. Sometimes they even accompanied him around town and follow him around with an entourage that visually proved his status.

As they approach the house as they entered, householder's clients and guests could move towards the right, walk toward the magnificent shrine, and make a small offering to the gods that are part of their household. This will help increase the wealth of the household and can help keep one's relationship with the housekeeper.

Shrine located in an atrium in the House of Menander

In the morning the householder would usually take a seat in the tablinum room, located adjacent to the atrium. It was used as an office and a place to sit with his clients (perhaps with possibility of a library to the left, when you walk through the table). When he sat in the room the family man was presented to the public. The street in front of him was a group of customers who depended upon his assistance. The backdrop to him from behind were the stunning gardens of his stunning residence. Everything on this axis of sight was a symbol of power and opulence.

The slaves of the householder could move from front to back of the home without disrupting the work of the tablinum office. They could do this by taking a stroll through the small passageway that was next towards the tablinum. This was a necessity throughout all day because slaves were required to run the household effectively in all aspects. Clients who visited the householder at the beginning of the day However, they would not often leave the office. With the exception of slaves and relatives the only people who could pass through the office were clients of the homeowner. They were usually those who ate with him, for example and would meet in the afternoon for a delicious dinner at 5:00 in the large dining room. In the dining room they could enjoy the views from the gardens. They could also stroll through the walkway that is a colonnaded one that runs through the garden. They can enjoy conversations, art installations on the walls, as well as the protection of the gods and the past ancestors (see the shrine located at the rear of the Peristyle).

A few of the house's protection abilities are statues of the dead ancestors

When you exit at the House of Menander, check to check whether you can find the House of the Ceii is open at 1.6.15. It's worth a visit, however it's usually closed.

To get to 13th location, walk to the west with Block 1.10 on your right and block 1.3 to your left. Once you get to the next intersection following that continue straight ahead with block 8.7 to your left. The first main entrance to your left (after an alleyway to the right) is 8.7.28 The Temple of Isis.

Location 13 Location 13: The Temple of Isis (8.7.28)

Before entering the temple, look for the memorial plaque on the entrance. It reads like this:

Numerius Celsinus Popidius, the son of Numerius with his own money,, restored to its original foundations Temple of Isis, which was destroyed by the earthquake. Thanks to his generosity at just six years young, the councilors accepted in their ranks free of charge.

The entranceway's inscription is above the entryway to Temple of Isis. Temple of Isis

This inscription relates to a case where a six-year-old boy donated money to the construction of the temple. The result was that the child was appointed an elected member of the municipal government. The truth is certain to be the following:

One man an enslaved slave, became incredibly wealthy as a freedman becoming a part of an elite group of sub-elite super-rich, known as the Augustales (on their behalf, refer to Tour 7).

* The man who was born would never be a civic councilor due to his having previously was an escaped slave. The son of the man was born free and thus was eligible to be a councilor in the civic sphere in the event that money helped pave the way to his advancement.

* His father donated money to construct The temple of Isis in exchange for granting the status of a councilor to his son despite the fact that the son was just the age of six.

* It is likely that the father instructed the child about how to cast his vote at the local council.

Plaques commemorating both the initials of the father son and the mother of the son were found inside the temple within the temple itself.

Temple of Isis was rebuilt following its literal destruction during the 62/63 earthquake. It was one of the first temples to be rebuilt and demonstrates the importance in Isis as the Egyptian goddess Isis to the inhabitants of Pompeii. Isis was considered to be the great goddess who improved people's lives by enhancing the quality of life for her followers today and assured their passage to a state of eternal life. Who would not like to have a connection with a god like this? !

The Temple of Isis, with the altar of sacrifice in the left in the foreground.

In the temple precincts sit before the high temple. In the temple, priests perform their rituals of purification. The altar to sacrifice animals (on the altar archaeologists have found the bones and ashes of sacrificed victims) is located to on the left side of stairs, close to the purgatoriumwhich is a small structure lined with beautiful white marble. It was here that the water was kept, which purportedly was sourced from the Nile river. Nile -- which is the equivalent to holy water used to cleanse priests. On the left side are the priest's bedrooms as well as the kitchen. The high temple is behind the ekklesiasteron or dining space. Temples typically featured dining spaces within their buildings. Beautiful paintings were hung on the walls, along with an idol or bust Isis near.

After leaving the temple, repeat your steps to the right when you leave the temple. When you arrive at an intersection at the beginning, turn left to stop at the entrance to the right, labeled 8.7.25.

Location 14 Location 14: Location 14: Temple of Jupiter Meilichios (or Asclepius) (8.7.25)

While it appears to be an unimportant location however, it was actually an important location in the history of Pompeians at least during the aftermath of the earthquake. In the 62/63 earthquake The temple of the god Jupiter located in the Forum was badly damaged. The situation had to be rectified quickly due to the fact that Jupiter was the main god in the Rome imperial order (together with the gods Juno as well as Minerva) and the reverence for Jupiter was believed as essential for the proper functioning within the Roman system. Because

Jupiter was no longer believed to be worshipped at his Temple located in the Forum the small area was designated as the location to worship Jupiter. It was believed as a temporary solution considering that Jupiter's shrine located in the Forum was getting rebuilt prior to the eruption of the year 79. However, for the next seventeen to a little over a decade, the area became the site of rituals of worship for the Roman High God.

15. Location: The Grand Theater (8.7.20), The Little Theater (8.7.19) and the Gladiators Barracks (8.7.16)

The three main features in Pompeii (two theaters as well as an open barracks for gladiators) are usually accessible in conjunction. Depending on how the Superintendent has arranged the flow between them it is possible to move between the two without needing to step back to the street.

The Small Theater

Then it was discovered that the front entrance of The Grand Theater was covered with graffiti. These graffiti aren't visible nowadays. Here are two examples:

* "Methe of Atella the slave of Cominia loves Chrestus. Let Venus of Pompeii smile happily on their faces and may they always be in peace" (CIL 4.2457).

* "I'm hurrying to see you! Salute my Sava. I'm trying to love you" (CIL 4.2414).

However, in contrast to these statements about love, one skeptic said these sarcastic lines: "It is a wonder, O Wall, that you're not shattered by the weight of all this absurdity" (CIL 4.2461).

Pompeians loved theatre. Theatrical masks were sprayed on the walls of homes throughout the town. This was especially true for the wealthy, who adored to appear at the theatre, and not only because it boosted their social standing. Both in the Grand Theater (which seated 5,000) as well as The Little Theater (which seated 1,000) You can observe the places where the elite and officials of the city sat in special seats towards the front (just like you would see at the Amphitheater). This was a method to remind them and everyone else of their significance. The Grand Theater, some of the town's most prominent people were also seated in the boxed sections both sides of the stage which gave them a better view of the stage and also allowing them to be seen by the general public.

A painting taken from an Pompeii residence that depicts the figure of a woman as well as a man with masks taken off

A mosaic made up of a group made up of performers (from The House of the Tragic Poet)

Then, in the Grand Theater, see if you can spot the location in which it was that the Marcus Holconius Rufus seat constructed. Here's the clue: Holconius Rufus was an significant benefactor to Pompeii and, therefore, his seat is located in the middle and towards the front. Holconius Rufus, along and his twin brother financed the vast improvements and renovations of the theater, as well as other town features during the time of the emperor Augustus. He wouldn't be alive enough to see his work being covered in Vesuvian Ash. There's also an archway in the most important intersection of Pompeii that is dedicated to his memory. Therefore, if you take his chair inside the Grand Theater, you'll be sitting in the seat of one of Pompeii's most famous inhabitants.

The seat inscription of Holconius Rufus that is encased in bronze, notes his importance: "Dedicated by decree of the town councilors in honor of Marcus Holconius Rufus the son of Marcus Duumvir who had five times judicial power and twice quinquennial duumvir military tribune on popular demand as well as a the priest of Augustus and the patron saint of the Colony."

Seat of Holconius at the Grand Theater

Pompeians were enthralled by gladiators. They were the hottest stars in the early century. Images and graffiti of them can be found all over Pompeii and sometimes in the tomb decorations.

Pompeii was the first city to dedicate a vast courtyard for the home and the training of gladiators. Gladiators were slaves under the control of their masters who were likely to have owned a group of gladiators. They could have trained in the barracks' courtyard and then had to compete against one another within the arena. The tiny rooms scattered around the courtyard served as their home. As the rooms were excavated they found skeletons in a few of the rooms. The skeletons contained chainlike iron and even fetters around their arms and legs and legs, which suggests that these gladiators were confined during the entire volcano of Vesuvius. Evidently , the people with the keys for unlocking the fetters were out of the city without a thought for the gladiators. Unchained skeletons of a couple were discovered in the guardroom. Helmets and body armor were discovered from the room. Excavators also observed that the columns surrounding the courtyard were adorned with alternate hues of yellow, red blue, and red, with blue being the only exception in the bottom, nonfluted portion of the columns that was red in every case.

The Gladiators' Barracks

In the barracks of the gladiators head to the south-facing end and look north to view the magnificent Grand Theater behind the barracks. Additionally, on one side, on the eastern end of the courtyard there are toilets.

The best way to move to your next destination is this. Locate the massive staircase located to the northwest of the barracks of the gladiators. After ascending these steps to the right, then left at the top. You will pass by an area known as Triangular Forum to your left, and shortly after there is you will see the Grand Theater on your right. (Notice that this is, in fact that the foundation on the so-called Doric Temple within the Triangular Forum. It's probably the oldest temple in Pompeii which dates back to 6100 years prior to the eruption of Vesuvius.) Once you are on the street, turn slightly to the left, then to proceed northwards and keep blocks 8.4 on your right , and block 8.5 to your left.

This is where you will find located on the Street of Abundance once again. For your next location, go to the north until you arrive at the second intersection, which is north on the street of Abundance. (It seems further than it actually is.)

Attention: The next venue is an infamous brothel. There are explicit sexual images that are painted over the interior walls. If the content you see is offensive to your guests it is possible to skip to 17th Avenue. 17. If that is the case, make a right turn along to the Street of Abundance.

When you arrive at the location 16 You will see to your left, a piece of exterior wall that is predominantly red. It is still possible to see the snakes' pattern throughout the painting. You've seen it in Tour 1, depicting snakes on walls was a method of imagining the good and positive spirits of the area. This painting was painted close to 7.11.12 that was a brothel that had only one room. When you look over the doorway, there is a phallic image likely to function as a sign of luck and also as an advert for the work of the small brothel.

16. Location: A Brothel (7.12.18)

In the years following finding Pompeii The only visitors permitted to visit the site were males. Women were not allowed to enter the Forum while men were permitted to see "the places of interest." This location is, however, not in need of explanation. The five rooms on the ground floor of the brothel were decorated with paintings showing the various services offered in the establishment. The beds made of stone would be covered with mattresses (perhaps made of straw) and pillows. The people who provided the services were mostly (but maybe not solely) women and it is likely that the majority were slaves. The toilet was situated at one end of the hallway and there were 5 more rooms on the upper floors (rarely accessible for tourists).

The room used for prostitution.

After leaving the brothel, it is important to return in your Street of Abundance. The superintendency recommends that guests exit the brothel via the back entrance and then join to the Street of Abundance from that direction, rather than returning to their original route. This is due to the fact that the street leading to the brothel not large enough to handle two-way traffic when the volume of tourists is large. Therefore, when you leave the back entrance at the back of the establishment, you must follow the narrow road with Block 7.11 to your left. This street runs to the left, before it meets it with Street of Abundance. Make a right turn along that Street of Abundance. In a short time, you'll get to your next destination (at 7.9.67). However, before you arrive try to discover the only other piece of artifact which is connected to the theme of this portion of your trip The phallic symbol appears from a stone within the road outside 7.13.3. It appears to be pointed in precisely in the direction that the brothel you have just went to. It could be that the symbol of luck doubles as a direction signal in this particular instance.

17th Location: The Street Fountain of Abundance (7.9.67)

The street fountain depicted in this video is a goddess female named Fortuna (or the goddess of abundance). She holds a cornucopia representing abundance. This is the reason that led archaeologists and archaeologists to name the road you've been strolling on this morning "Abundance" not due to the many eateries and shops that line the route, but rather because this fountain in the street represents the god Fortuna with her cornucopia of abundance.

The fountain on the street of Fortuna just in right in front of the rear entryway to the Eumachia Building

The fountain behind the street The entrance 7.9.67 leads to the staircase that rises to the top of the hill from the road. The structure that is accessible via the staircase was significant in the early centuries and you can find out much more within Tour 4. The back of the building has an inscription on it. A more extensive version of that inscription was originally affixed to columns that were high above the Forum however, that one is in a state of decay. This is what the inscription says:

Eumachia was the daughter of Lucius the public priestess in her own name, and in the name of her son Marcus Numistrius fronto, built on her own funds the Chalcidicum [i.e. the front vestibule), the crypt, and the portico [that's the covered walkway with a colonnaded designto honor Augustan Concord and Piety, and dedicated them.

There are a few things that need to be made clear about the inscription. Firstof all, the principal person who donated the massive structure in the name of a town, was actually a female named Eumachia. It is likely that she have been a major public figure who served as a patron to the town with her huge financial reserves. There is more evidence for this assumption on both Tour 4 and Tour 7 (when you visit her huge tomb). But for now take note of the fact that the public benefactor wasn't a male. We also know of female patrons of Pompeii also -- such as Mamia who's tomb will be revealed upon entering the Forum.

The second, Eumachia's structure had been dedicated "Augustan Concord as well as Piety." It was believed that the term "piety" meant giving the proper respect to everyone and especially to Gods. The term "concord" was the establishment of harmonious relations between the various cities that were often competing with one another. Also, what Eumachia promoted in her writings was the creation of proper relationships with the gods as well as with other people. It is interesting that the fact this program was assigned to the Emperor Augustus is a sign of the high expectations for the empire which arose after Augustus's rule as the emperor.

When you approach the Forum take note of the following. Of Pompeii's 11,000 wall and graffiti inscriptions one was painted red on the outside wall in the Building of Eumachia. The inscription said: "The gladiatorial troupe of Aulus Suettius Certus Aedile will battle in Pompeii on May 31.

It will include a hunt as well as the aprons" (CIL 4.1189). The exact same message was painted on the wall near the brothel. The civic official was the one who supported his own group of gladiators and wanted the public to be aware of his kindness to the town and the people.

The second is where the Eumachia building joins the Forum Notice the differences in the building materials of the wall that runs along the Street of Abundance in which the bigger and white bricks are matched by small and more red bricks. The entire area was covered in plaster, which some of is still visible today. However, the distinction between the two kinds of construction materials can be due to the 62/63 earthquake. The quake was a major cause of destruction to the Forum and all over the town. In this case, the portion of the building that faced the Forum was required to be rebuilt entirely. We can see the stunning bricks, purchased from Eumachia along with her husband on the right hand side, and the bricks that are less impressive, likely paid for by the town on the left.

Two different construction styles Pre-dating (left) as well as the post-dating (right) and the earthquakes of the years 62/63.

Also, take note of the three massive stones that block access for carts entering the Forum. The ideal was that this Forum wasn't a spot for dirty mules or tradesmen. This was the place where one could be treated with humility, respect for others and civic obligation. Now you are in Pompeii, the heartbeat of Pompeii.

Chapter 7: Southern Water Sides

This short excursion will take you to the waterfronts of Pompeii. Since it was a harbor city the water fronts of Pompeii provided Pompeii with the features which boosted the economy of Pompeii more than other.

For your aid in orienting yourself with respect to where you'll be This map will help you navigate of the four destinations on the tour's third (Locations 18-21, beginning at the 17th location of the previous tour).

If you're able to do only the half-day tour due to time limitations You should focus specifically on Location 20 especially. Toilets are available near the river's entry point of Location 19.

To go to the next location on this tour from Location 17 walk east across the Forum to reach the main road that leads away from the Forum towards the southwest. The entrance on your right (7.7.32) leads to Temple of Apollo that you will go to at the conclusion of the tour. After that, you'll take the first entrance on your left. Alternately, if you're able to gain access to Location 18 directly from the Forum (a way that's normally blocked because of construction, but is expected to open one day) then you'll be entering it the same way that most people used to do in the days before it was erupted of 79.

Location 18 Pompeii's Basilica

Built around 100 BCE Pompeii's basilica was the oldest basilica that remains in Italy. The building was where Pompeians came to for transactions with the business to be recorded legally or in the event of legal disputes. Its primary purpose was that it functioned as an office for the court. Magistrates who heard the cases of the local population were sitting in the covered courtroom that you can still view today. The only thing you are unable to see is the roof , which could have covered the entire of the basilica. It was held in place by massive central columns. On these columns and the walls archaeologists have found a substantial amount of graffiti (which are no longer in existence).

The tribunal that is situated at the western part of the basilica

After you have left the basilica, go west , and then turn left to enter the next entrance to your left.

Location 19 the Temple of Venus and the River Harbor

There's not much to discover here, as there was once a grand temple dedicated to Pompeii's protector goddess, Venus. The earthquake of 1962/63 caused it's damage in this area and, at the time of the eruption the temple had not been fully rebuilt. Prior to the earthquake the temple was beautiful situated at the top of the town, with a view of the harbors of the river and the sea that surrounded the town. It was the ideal location to be Venus to be worshiped - as the location in which she could supervise the primary economic stimulant for the town from the water below.

While the temple wasn't yet fully restored as of when the volcano erupted however, it was being renovated, and the foundation on the site was being extended to create a more stunning temple to Venus Pompeiana, and a temple that was more visible from the water, as ships were entering the harbors.

A few Pompeian artwork depicts Venus naked in poses. In one of the residences, she was shown naked on an oyster. In another instance, she appears to be washing her hair not dressed (a pose that was replicated in the nearby fountain on the street in Herculaneum). These images are not sly as scenes depicted in brothels. These intimate images of the city's patron god with a comfortable posture could be a way to prove that Venus found herself at home under the shade of the mountain Vesuvius.

Venus is at ease at home in the Vesuvian region

The pathway through the Temple of Venus will lead you to steps that lead down to the southwest end that is the site of the temple. On this pathway, you can be able to see the impressive buildings which used to provide views across the harbor of Pompeii on the Sarno River (including the Sarno Baths with their impressive arches that are visible on the other wall's edge). You can also imagine the river in your own imagination. The river may be flowing beyond the boundaries of the site as it is today. The flat, flat land within the site might be used to create this harbor area. It is easy to imagine the bustling harbor, filled with vessels, ships dock workers, shipmen carts, and harbor workers. It was an extremely bustling place.

If any of your guests is in need of restrooms, there are toilets that are accessible to the public in the structures which allow access to Pompeii at the moment.

To reach the next destination take a stroll around the southwest town walls and keep the walls to your left. At the time of the eruption the walls had gone through their initial defensive functions that were so crucial in the beginning of the Roman settlement of this town.

While you travel around the walls to the southwest corner of the town, you'll soon be at the western entrance gate to Pompeii. It is here that you be required to show your ticket to a person at a turnstile gate. (Your ticket functions as a daily pass, which means you should have no issue going through this gate, and getting into the town from the western end.) Once you've passed at the entrance, you must take the steps to your left, in order to descend to the 20th location.

20th Location: The Suburban Baths and Sea Harbor

The Suburban Baths

Before entering into the Suburban Baths, look to the left as you walk along the wall that runs to the north from Bath Complex. There are numerous anchoring points protruding off the walls. When they were first discovered in 1950s, they were believed to be mooring points for the ships that were moored within the harbor of the sea. However, they would be too high above sea level for this reason. They would have probably served a sea-related reason, but we are unable to know their exact purpose. They could have secured harnesses and ropes that were used to secure cargo from ships of the sea that docked in Pompeii.

Mooring points that are used for maritime reasons

Enter The Suburban Baths, which were built to a excellent standard in the reign of the Emperor Tiberius (emperor between 14 and 1937). Bathing facilities were widespread throughout The Roman world. They were places where people could be seen in particular in the afternoons. Elites would gather in bathing facilities to relax, clean as well as exercise and sports (if they had a palaestra, something this one doesn't). There are three additional baths during the tour following the Forum and Central Baths, all of they were perfectly placed to serve the inhabitants in Pompeii (the Forum, Central as well as the Stabian Baths). There is no doubt that the Suburban Bath was also utilized by the locals, but they also have the perfect location for catering to ships that docked in Pompeii's harbors.

Similar to the admission fee to get into Pompeii in the first century, people of the first century paid a fee for entry into to the 2-story Suburban Baths. Bath complexes typically had female and male sections however, this does not appear to be the case with The Suburban Baths. It is possible that this bath was geared exclusively to males.

Customers would change their clothes inside the room for changing (or the apodyterium). It is easily located within the Suburban Baths. The room has eight scenes of erotica that are painted on the walls, with Roman numerals outlined beneath the scenes. It's fun to imagine these were among the items that were on the menu for sexual offerings that were offered by the bath facility. However, they could have had a more practical use at the very most in the beginning. The room was fitted with boxes which were placed on tables (just as the boxes with numbers painted on the walls below the erotic pictures). The customer would place his clothing in one of those boxes and then place them beneath some of the 8 images while bathing experience. If he went back for his clothing, he'd be able to pinpoint the box that contained his clothes , by recollecting the erotic photo underneath which it was set.

However, it is possible that the photos could have served a secondary purpose also. There is a good chance that the suspicion is that a brothel could be operating at the second level of these facilities There is no doubt that other images could serve the same purpose of tracking down one's belongings like landscape or nautical scenes. Also, it's probable that these pictures were used to promote the potential that were ahead for sailors who recently docked following a trip in the sea.

After removing their clothes, clients moved through three rooms. First, there was the frigidarium used for bathing in cold water, which was intended to increase the body's attention to the temperature. Then, there was the tepidarium where the bathing water was at moderate temperatures. The caldarium then immersed the client in hot water similar to the sauna. The three rooms following are identical to the same standard but with two unique aspects. The first is that the frigidarium expands into a second room that houses stunning scenic paintings as well as an erupting fountain dedicated to the god Mars. In addition, the caldarium benefitted from a semi-circular wall that had three windows, which looked out towards the ocean.

The god Mars is depicted as the form of a fountain that cascades down

Beyond the caldarium is a room with the hypocaust floor. The hot water used in the caldarium was derived from the fires, which were also used to heat the air through an hypocaust heating device that was used for baths. This meant raising the floors to let hot air circulate beneath the floor. They were held on their edges by brick pillars, which let them be suspended from hollow spaces where hot air flowed.

Beyond the caldarium, there is a huge area of pool, which leads to the small anteroom that you leave the building.

To reach the next destination, turn left along the narrow street that leads back to the Forum. The Forum will be entered into Pompeii via The Marine Gate. As you approach the area where the street begins to level off, you will notice the white marble insertions in the paving stones along the street. Perhaps it was a means to increase the awe-inspiringness of the city for those who had just entered the city via some of the harbour areas. It could be as if spreading in the carpet of red to the visitors. Perhaps because the marble inserts sit between the Temples of Venus to the left of the street and Apollo to the left that runs along the streets, maybe they heightened the feeling that gods are revered and honored here, with the divinities blessing it with lavishness.

The next destination Temple of Apollo will be on your left when you reach 7.7.32.

Place 21 The Temple of Apollo (7.7.32)

The altar (foreground) is located in the Temple of Apollo (with sundial on the left side of the altar)

The temple isn't usually accessible to the general public, however should it be accessible when you go to the town, be lucky. It was dedicated to Greek god Apollo which is the most important god within the Greek gods' system. Apollo was the god of light, and it's only appropriate that a sundial sits within the shrine (standing on a high platform just to the left on the right side of the principal altar when you enter it from the road). In a way this Temple of Apollo is more in line to the Forum Tour as the majority of its time, it would have been in contact to the Forum. At the end of Pompeii's existence, however there was a wall constructed which gave the temple the impression of being a separate entity, decreasing the perception that it was one of Forum complex.

Apollo within the temple of Apollo (from 2 angles)

The transition to Tour 4

You'll need to figure out how to organize the following portion in your schedule. If you have time it is best to take on Tour 4 now, the Forum tour (which may take around approximately 20 minutes) and then lunch. Or, you could choose to eat your lunch right now and then return to Tour 4 after that. If you want to eat lunch prior to taking the tour around the Forum There is a cafeteria which is accessible just after the northern edge on the Forum. The Forum tour begins by focusing on the temple at north-western side of the Forum -the Temple of Jupiter.

Chapter 8: The Forum

This brief tour takes you to the major buildings that surround that courtyard, which is part of the Forum. Cities in the Roman world had almost always an important central forum with important buildings surrounding the forum. These buildings brought together judicial, commercial and political activities to one central location and accentuated the way that the distinctions in our contemporary world merged in the world of ancient times.

For you to help you find your way on the road to the places you'll be traveling For your convenience, here's an outline of the eight destinations of the 4th tour.

If you're unable to do the entire tour due to limitations in time, then concentrate on the locations 23-26. There are restrooms right outside the Forum in the north in the cafeteria. they will be there when you've completed this short trip.

The enumerators that are used for specific locations are not very helpful in this tour, as this tour is about huge structures. For instance The temple built by Jupiter is listed by number 7.8.1. Because the temples are easily visible and easily accessible, it's more efficient simply to list their locations instead of listing their location specific enumerators. The only exception could be Location 29, which requires an enumerator (7.4.16).

On this tour, your attention will be on the Forum in the clockwise direction. It will begin at the center point to the northern end of the Forum which is it is known as the Temple of Jupiter.

The location 22 The Temple of Jupiter

The Temple of Jupiter with Vesuvius in the background

In the middle of the Forum towards its northern apex is in the northern part of the Forum is the Temple of Jupiter. The shrine was constructed to honor three main Rome gods -three gods namely Jupiter, Juno, and Minerva. Jupiter was the god of the highest rank for Roman gods. Roman state, and it's fitting to note that the inhabitants of Pompeii put it in right in the middle of the Forum.

A head from Jupiter is a sculpture inside the Pompeian temple (now resting on a bench that is just above the temple's platform)

The next one is located to the right to the right of the Temple of Jupiter in the northeast part of the Forum.

Area 23 Macellum

Three pillars which were originally part of the Forum's colonnade are the gateway into the macellum. In front of them is two entrances with arched openings that lead to the precinct. It was a meat and fish market. The twelve stones that were in central part of the complex served as poles for awnings that gave shade to the central portion that was the place for the sale. Archaeologists have discovered massive amounts of bones of fish in this area. Another place for selling meats and fish was the room on right of the building's rear of the buildingit was a room with three counters for selling products.

The middle room to the back, which has the white steps of marble, has two statues that are encased in niches. Although they were originally believed to be a representation of members from the family of Emperors the likelihood is they represent the benefactors that helped to fund the renovation of the macellum following the earthquake -- likely the husband and wife of a man. Their generosity ensured the prestige of their family, and these statues were intended to guarantee the longevity of the family's honor.

The husband and wife might have funded the renovation of the Macellum

The room on the back left features two white marble podiums. While we can't be certain of the purpose it was used for religious ceremonies as well as banquets.

Before leaving the macellum, it is likely that you'll be tempted to take a look at the artwork located on the west wall which depicts a mystical collection of scenes. In the beginning, it was vibrant in color, this stunning panel is now extremely faded.

After leaving the building, take a left. You'll pass through three entrances, leading to small areas. The first two were stores. The third one was home to an altar for the gods however only the base of the altar is visible. The next site is the large opening in the next entrance.

24-hour location: The Temple of the Genius of the Region

While the area appears uninteresting, it nevertheless had a vital function and was evident by its size. It was the place where people was dedicated to the spirit or power of the area. It may sound odd to many in the 21st century However, the ancient perspective frequently believed that the area had an element of spirituality (as we've already witnessed in various places in the course of our travels). This spiritual dimension functioned in conjunction with the material dimension of the space. If the spiritual dimension of the location wasn't nurtured it, the physical dimension of the space was weakened. In the event that the energy of the area was healthy, then good things happened to the physical dimensions of the area. Thus, the citizens of Pompeii created a vast area to increase the reverence for the divine or the creative spirit of the area. This was more crucial following the earthquake, in order to make sure that another catastrophe like this would not again occur to the city.

Once you're in a position to go on take a stroll south and continue to the next entrance, which is located on the eastern edge of the Forum. Forum.

Location 25 The Temple of Vespasian, the Emperor. Vespasian

The small entryway to the building was decorated with marble at moment of eruption. When you walk into the structure, you're going through a separate temple precinct. The main features and the platform of the temple were decorated with marble. The temple was very impressive at the moment when the volcano began. The temple was being restored when the eruption in the year 79. Archaeologists have discovered in the northern wall that it had only received the first coat of stucco; the final coat was not yet put on.

The most fascinating part of the temple is the altar made of marble that is visible for the entire world to view. The four sides of the altar depict scenes of sacrifice. In front of the entrance into Temple is perhaps the most fascinating side of all four (the west side). We can see an ongoing sacrificial ritual. Priests wear a toga that covers his head -- a typical image of the role of a priest. He pours a sacrificial sacrifice in a bowl to the altar. A variety of people gather around the priest on his left. On the right side are the butcherand his attendant and the animal to be killed -- a common sacrifice to honor an the emperor.

The marble front altar of the Temple of the Emperor Vespasian

The other three sides contribute to the sacrificial symbolism of the marble altar. To the northern side there is an oblong, a ladle and a pitchereach of which was used as ceremonial objects during sacrifices. On the south side , there is an altar cloth and a staff, along with an incense container which enhanced the offering to the gods. On the east, on that side depicting the sacrifice of the bull is a marble with an oak leaf wreath in between two laurels. These were symbols of the Imperial Empire which suggests that the temple was dedicated to the Emperor. The inscription on the temple suggests that a famous citizen recently gave the emperor Tiberius and this is likely to be that temple. Prior to that, the site was home to an ancient temple known as the Temple of the Genius of Augustus which was the location to honor the god of the great Emperor from The Roman the imperial lineage. Following the quake of 62/63 the site was redesigned to honor the current emperor in of the forum's precincts.

Location 26 The Eumachia Building

The final building located on the eastern end of the Forum is the enormous Eumachia Building. The white marble facade that surrounds the entrance could not belong to the building. The archaeologists believed that it did , and then forced it to be as aesthetically pleasing as they could. However, we now believe that they put this on the wrong place. It is not known what it was at the time of the eruption. We do know that it was on some of the Forum structures.

The same inscription as you observed above the back entrance to the Eumachia building (by the fountain of Abundance) was seen at the top of pillars that ran along the outside colonnade of to the entrance of Eumachia building, looking towards the Forum. It was a declaration of Augustan Concord and piety. Some of the Forum are still clearly visible, either lying in the earth or being repositioned above the pillars which originally stood in their place. Eumachia ensured that her construction and, consequently, her name could be tapped into the core ideological elements that comprised the Roman imperial order. Concord and piety made sure that peace and security were guaranteed.

Eumachia encouraged the civil concord of the Augustan period.

It is bolstered by other elements of the structure as well as external features. Take a look at the exterior first. Examine the semicircular apse that is to left of the entrance to Eumachia's house. On either end of the apse, there are two niches, as well as two inscriptions resided at lower part within the niches. The right-hand inscription is clearly visible, however it's a replica of the original. The one on the left isn't visible. The inscriptions honored two of Rome's greatest heroes. Above them, were statues of these heroes. The two heroes are Aeneus on the left side of the niche, and Romulus on the right. Both were major characters in Roman mythology, relating to the origins of Rome as the city that will never die and blessed by the gods.

The apse that lies to right of entryway into the Eumachia Building, with two niches that are dedicated to Aeneus (left) and Romulus (right)

The inscription on Romulus (CIL 10.809) stated Romulus to be the child of deity Mars and stated it was believed that Romulus was "received in the gods" when he died. The inscription for Aeneas isn't as well preserved.

The Romulus inscription declared him "among the group of gods" (in deoru[mthe deity's name)

The main feature inside that bolstered Roman imperial philosophy was a statue that was situated on the central pedestal, which was located in front of the main entrance on the opposite side of the structure. This pedestal housed an idol of the female god Concordia Augusta (the concord brought by Augustus) So, as the inscriptions that were placed at the entrances were strengthened by this statue, which was placed at the centre of the courtyard's central area.

Furthermore this statue Concordia Augustus was designed to resemble Livia who was his wife. Augustus and wife of his son Emperor

Tiberius. Livia was a strong and influential woman, who Eumachia was likely to seek to imitate. It's fitting, therefore that just behind the statue of Concordia Augusta there is a second niche in the rear of the building devoted for the display of Eumachia.

Statue of Eumachia

The inscription that is beneath the statue of Eumachia is a tribute to "Eumachia the granddaughter of Lucius, public priestess." The statue was created by the association or guild of laundry workers (the fullers) who indicated their dedication to her by writing her name on the inscribed. Eumachia was then an benefactor to the group of launderers (and possibly to other associations too). Even though she was barred from taking public office on due to her sexuality, Eumachia and other women with financial resources could have had a significant influence via their support of organizations.

The Eumachia Building was a part of an enormous rectangular courtyard that was bordered by corridors that ran along the outside. What did these spaces serve for? Many have suggested that they could be used to wash clothes. We've already seen those who were fullers or laundry people paid for the statue and inscription in honor of Eumachia in this location. Also, what appears to be the urinal was found near the entry point of the structure (on the right side as you enter) This suggests that some kind of washing may have been conducted here, because urine contains ammonia, which helps to remove impurities of the cloth.

The best perspective is, however, that the building was likely utilized for various reasons, but washing clothes could be just one of them. The building could have been a primarily rental space, which would have allowed a variety of different activities to take place there, in various designs and at various dates. Perhaps it was a space for selling on the market. In reality, we can think that slave trading was a major practice that took place in the premises. Merchants could have brought their slaves to the premises and sold them to people who needed additional support in their households. The slaves were the electric force of the old world and kept the society alive. There was not much thought about morality.

After leaving your departure from the Eumachia Building, head to the southern end of the Forum just in front of that of the Temple of Jupiter.

Location 27 the Civic Administrative Buildings

The central of the southern portion of the Forum is the three bays which directly are facing to the Temple of Jupiter. Although it's not completely specific what these structures were intended to serve but the most reliable hypothesis is that they assisted in the storage and recording of town records. Town scribes were employed in these bays, and the documents would have been kept in the buildings that were above and behind these bays, and civic officials could have had Council meetings within one bay. In the central bay, an inscription was discovered which identified the Emperor Augustus in the title of "son of God."

The west side of the administrative structures to the west of these administrative buildings was (1) one small house, which was followed by (2) more grander homes that could have offered stunning views of the Sarno River and the river harbor.

Then, proceed north along the western part of the Forum and pass by to the Temple of Apollo on the left. As you travel, note the resemblance with (1) The two story columns in white marble on at the Temple of Apollo in the Forum as well as (2) an artifact discovered in the possession belonging to Julia Felix (from Tour 1). The painting shows residents from Pompeii reading a notice for the public that is hung before three statues of men riding horses, and there are two stories of columns behind the statues. The scene that the artist from Pompeii has depicted exactly to what we see in the Forum and even in our day.

The painting is of the House of Julia Felix, showing residents reading a sign in Pompeii's Forum

Area 28 The Measuring Table

After passing by after passing the Temple of Apollo on your left, you'll come to a measuring table to your left. It was a weigh station that controlled the selling of goods according to standard measurements (like the famous first century saying in Matthew 7:2 "with the measure you employ to measure it, it is measured for the measurement you use"). The nine different basins featured a drain at the bottom , which could be closed to measure , and then removed to allow the contents to escape.

The measuring table

To the north of this table is a structure that could be a granary that was used to sell cereals. The building is now storage space. It is worth a moment to check out what's on display in your visit.

Make your way from the Forum by crossing the gate to the northeast end of the Forum (between the Temple of Jupiter and the macellum). This will take you to the last stop of the tour.

Location 29 the Neighborhood Shrine towards Jupiter (7.4.16)

Take a stand in the middle of the entryway to 7.4.16 This is an apartment on the corner. What the residence was used for is not clear. It could have been an workshop to members of an organization, an establishment for wine or a pottery store.

It is not disputed however that gods were displayed on the external facade of this building. On the left pillar , there was an image of Mars the god of the war. His left hand was holding an armoury and his right hand was holding an iron spear. The painting has been ruined by the forces of nature.

The deity that is on the right pillar is visible, though not as clearly. The god is located inside an altar that was built to enhance your security in the area. The shrine is a representation of Jupiter as the primary god of the Forum and the highest god in that of the Roman empire. In the shrine Jupiter's left hand is holding the Scepter (to his right) as his right is holding the thunderbolt (to his left).

Together, the two gods help to recount important elements of the Roman imperial story and the gods of war and power have helped establish Rome's eternal rule.

The transition to Tour 5

The cafeteria and restrooms are located across the street towards the west and just south of the Temple of Jupiter. The fifth tour starts at this point.

Chapter 9: The Northwest Sector

Most likely, you've just had your lunch and taken an afternoon of relaxation in the cafeteria along with your friends. It is likely that you're now rested for this trip that will guide you to some Pompeii's most intriguing sites to the northwest region of the town.

To aid you in orienting yourself with respect to the place you'll be traveling to get you there, a diagram of all six destinations on the 5th tour can be found here.

On this tour, you'll be covering quite a bit of terrain. If you are unable to complete all of the tour due to the time limitations, then you should focus on the locations 30 and 32 as well as 33. Toilets are available at the final point on the trip (at 35). If you are concerned that you may be running out of time, you may have decide whether you want to finish the tour in Tour 5 or Tour 6 or leave Tour 7 for your exit from Pompeii.

If you're ready to start, you can leave the cafeteria and head left. The first three entrances on the left will open up into shops.

The fourth entrance is 7.5.24 The first place you will visit on the tour.

Area 30 The Forum Baths (7.5.24)

For us, the term "bath" is associated with the image of a tub within a small space. For people from the ancient world of the Greco-Roman the word "bath" had an entirely different meaning. Bathing facilities were a huge (and at times, a huge) facility that met the needs of the culture and social of the residents. Naturally the bodies of people were washed in the baths' waters. baths, however, baths weren't just a place to clean dirt and grime prior to returning to the outside world. Baths were, in many ways, the primary point of life in the city as interaction between the residents being encouraged within bath complexes. Political, social and economic bonds among individuals were strengthened there as the hierarchy of social the differentiating of people's status were continuously examined there. Also, entertainment and recreation were also provided. Every person who was a member of the society was sure to go to the baths sometime during the daytime. Most men would gather there for hours in afternoons. The majority of baths for women offered separate facilities. If baths did not offer separate female facilities the women would have gathered to the baths in the early morning (unless there was a reason why the facilities were thought to be only for men as was the case with Baths in the Suburban Area of Tour 3). Suburban Baths of Tour 3).

Forum Baths Forum Baths were initially constructed to be a one-stop bathing facility however, during the reign of Emperor Augustus an additional section was created to allow women to bathe apart from, and concurrently with men. It was smaller and less elaborate than the men's bathing area. It also had an external courtyard where the guys could run around. The men's area is typically accessible to the public.

The majority of the water reserve for the bath complex was stored in enormous tanks within the adjoining blocks in Pompeii (in Block 7.6 and 7.6.17), which was accessible by 7.6.17 or 7.6.18). At their lowest, the tanks measured 16 feet by 49 feet. They were taller from 30 to 40 feet. They could have held 430,000 liters, or

113,000 Gallons of water once they were fully filled.

The concept is to build Forum Baths. Forum Baths (not all of these areas are accessible to visitors)

The women's and men's sections were comprised of three rooms which had significantly different temperatures within these rooms. This effect was caused by the cooling and heating of air and water. Central boiler systems was used to heat the air and water and air, which were then moved in stages, with sections for men on one side , and the women's section on the other. The caldarium, or hot room was located closest to the boiler, and it received more heat. The heated air and water was then channeled to the warm room, or the tepidarium and later into the frigidarium, or cold room after it had lost its warmth.

If the water flow and air changed from cold to hot and vice versa, those who took baths would go in opposite directions. In the beginning, they would soak them in the colder water. The cooler water in that section will awaken their senses. After you've passed through the men's changing room The frigidarium is the first room you'll see. The pool is situated in central part of the space featuring two marble levels which could serve as seats or steps. Bathers may also be seated within the niches in the room and chat. The reddish cornice over the niches portrays cupids riding horses or Chariots.

The men's tepidarium of the Forum Baths. Forum Baths

The second area is the one called the tepidarium with beautiful ceilings. The temperature of this room was much cooler, assisted partly by the installation of the bronze brazier heater that was located on the opposite end of the room. It came with three benches that allowed bathers to take in the warmth close. They were given by a gentleman named Marcus Nigidius Vaccula, as his name was engraved on the heaters with the words "at his own cost." The idea was to use it as a great opportunity to market his name to the urban dwellers who frequented the Forum Baths every day. The benefactor was a jolly person. This is evident in an image of a cow positioned in the middle of the heater. The name Vaccula is "little cow."

The brazier heater as well as the bench and Vaccula's cow at the middle of the heater

After getting up to sweat inside the hot tub bathers would head to the caldarium with its stunning ceiling made comprised of smooth, ribbed cement. Take note of the hot bath on one side of the room, constructed from white marble. These were the same as saunas from the first century (although the water wasn't circulated by motorized pumps that were high-pressure). They were not cesspools for disease. Each hot bath included a drain pipe which allowed the old water to be drained. This was necessary to ensure that the water was maintained at a high temperature. The impurities that were accumulating up in the bath should also have been eliminated in the process. The drainpipe is visible on the right-hand side of the bath.

The other end of the caldarium is there is a huge marble basin located in the apse of the room. It is surrounded by plenty of light emanating from skylights. Within the rim of this basin, there are marble inserts which identify the two people who contributed to the gift, and highlighting their significance to everyone to view. Inscription (CIL 10.817) says: "Gnaeus Melissaeus Aper (son of Gnaeus) and Marcus Staius Rufus (son of Marcus) elected officials, with judicial authority twice was responsible for the creation of the basin through a an order of town councillors at costs of the public. It cost 5,250 sesterces."

The basin of the caldarium with arched arches

Once you've finished your trip to Forum Baths Forum Baths, you will likely exit the baths by retracing your steps, and exiting through the same doorway you have entered. (Occasionally the exit to the north is accessible however from my experience, it typically isn't.) After exiting the baths, make a left and continue towards the next street intersection. Location 31 is on your right side, just before the intersection.

Location 31 The Temple of Augustan Fortuna

While the temple is no longer stunning in its appearance, before the eruption, it was stunningly decorated with columns, steps and platforms made out of marble white. A single inscription (CIL 10.820) provides three facts concerning the temple. (1) It was commissioned through Marcus Tullius "at his own cost"; (2) it was located "on his land" as well (3) the temple was "the Temple of Augustan Fortuna." The goddess Fortuna was a goddess of protection and her protection was tied with the fates of Emperor Augustus and the imperial family who was a part of his lineage.

The Temple of Augustan Fortuna

Then turn left, and follow the road that runs along the north side of the Forum Baths. By crossing over to the opposite side, you'll come at the front door of The House of the Tragic Poet at 6.8.3.

Location 32 the House of the Tragic Poet (6.8.3/5)

The plans is that of House of the Tragic Poet

At 6.8.3 At 6.8.3, you're gazing into the famous House of the Tragic Poet. The reason behind its fame is the fact that it is at your feet, and looking at you with a glare -the famous dog from Pompeii. Under him is the Latin expression Cave Canem (pronounced "caw-way ca-nem").

It's tempting to believe that the phrase is simply "beware from the dog" however, this particular mosaic was not meant to warn anyone who was passing by that a dog like this lived within the household, but advise them to leave. People of the first century wanted their homes to be centers of activity in order to increase their standing; the greater the number of people in the house are in the house, the more important is the person who was living there. This was not meant to dissuade people from the house. In fact, as we witnessed in the House of Paquius Proculus (1.7.1) on Tour 1, it signaled that the home was protected by an animal spirit -- one that was that was as strong, loyal and possibly aggressive as a dog could have been in the real world. The people who were invited into the house were aware that spirits of great power had been asked to guard the home and its inhabitants. Therefore, this dog's mosaic acts as a home security tool to defend the home against evil spiritual forces.

The dog at the entrance mosaic in the House of the Tragic Poet

In the 21st century is to go through the back of the house However, before you go towards the rear, take note of how the visual axis the house allows a person who is walking by to look into the back of the home. You've probably observed this in other homes and will see more of it once the time is up. The eye is attracted by the shrine located in the rear of the house in which some of the gods that were part of the household were displayed. The family's devotion to God is portrayed to enhance its standing, and adding another level of security to any activity that took place within the home.

At the entrance of the home from the front, it could be possible to catch an image of the gorgeous artwork which was painted on the rear wall of the house. Actually, there were beautiful artworks throughout the entirety of the gorgeously decorated home.

If you haven't yet moved to the rear of the house make the move now by shifting towards the southeast corner, and going right until you come to the first entrance to the left. The entryway is likely to have been constructed by cutting down the size of the bedroom which is adjacent to it on the right when you go through the doorway. The back entrance could be the entrance to service to the dining and kitchen. The guests would never have required to enter this doorway. Their entrance was in front of the home.

There are many things to be aware of regarding the rear of the house. The first is the tiny Peristyle garden. This home was constrained by its size However, its owner created a stunning tiny garden inside his property. The peristyle's three sides allowed visitors to relax without feeling the tightness of the area. On the wall that was in the back of the garden, were six works depicting tragic scenes from the Greco-Roman mythology.

A truly powerful and stunning paintings of the entire city of Pompeii can be seen in this gallery (currently displayed in the National Archaeology Museum of Naples). It shows the young girl Iphigenia being carried away (unwillingly) in order to sacrifice to win the favor of gods and guarantee victory in an Greek naval war. Iphigenia is shown appealing to her father Agamemnon to help her. He turns his back in sorrow over the necessity of her murder but not doing anything to prevent her death for the good of all. (Various different versions of the tale exist which means that the slaughter of Iphigenia is not the final conclusion.)

The death that was made by Iphigenia of her House of the Tragic Poet (MANN 9112)

In the second, look at the exquisitely painted dining room with additional mythological scenes painted on the walls. The gardens and the garden shrine can be seen from the front entryway and the dining room has an identical perspective from a closer distance, but on the opposite axis. The space itself is spacious compared to the size of the home. The beautiful room could be utilized by the housekeeper and his guests at dinner. However, it's possible that this space was rented out to groups known as association (which were very common in the early 20th century) which allowed the members to gather and dine in a comfortable setting in the beauty of the surrounding.

Thirdly, you should be aware of the small space that was adjacent to the dining room. The tiny space was home to both the kitchen and toilet (no no longer visible, but it was directly to the right when you entered). In the early years, people weren't aware of the dangers of mixing cooking and human waste in the same place. The two-room arrangement can be found in the Vesuvian cities in Pompeii as well as Herculaneum.

After leaving the home take a retraced route towards the main road, then turn left. Continue past the stunning House of Maius at 6.6.1 then proceed to the next site at 6.6.21.

The location 33 The Bakery located in Insula Arriana Poloiana (6.6.17/20/21)

The design of the bakery is 6.6.17/20/21

There were around thirty bakeries within Pompeii that were of various size. When you enter the entryway of 6.6.21 You are facing the shopfront of one of the largest Bakeries in Pompeii. The space was where baked items were displayed. It is likely that we can imagine three or four persons working to make bread.

to passers-by at this busy street-corner. Much of the traffic moving into or out of the northwest section of the town would have passed by this bakery, and its two shop entryways give it superb access to potential customers. (Despite appearances, the smaller entryway toward the back wall on the left did not provide access from the street into the shop; instead, it was an entrance to a staircase that accessed the apartments above the bakery shop. The same was true for the small entryway next to it, just beyond the wall as you look north.)

A Pompeii painting of bread being distributed

Walk further back into the bakery complex. Three rooms separate the front shop from the oven room at the back. One of the smaller rooms seems to have been the kitchen where the household's food was prepared. The larger room that opens onto the street facilitated the feed bins that fed the mules needed to operate the bakery (see below). Found in that room was the skeleton of a mule that had been unable to escape its confines during the eruption of Vesuvius.

The oven room itself would have been a busy place. The activity would have gravitated around the oven and the large millstones. The baker or his slave would have poured wheat grains into the top of the millstones. The top millstones would then have been turned by slaves or by harnessed mules — using a wooden wedge placed through the square opening. This turning motion forced the grain to descend between the stones, breaking up the grain into fine flour, which would appear on the flat bench and be useable for baking.

A millstone for grinding wheat

The back room served as a bread preparation room. The dough was prepared on tables before being taken to the oven.

The oven in this bakery had two special features. To the right of the oven, above the area for two circular tubs (for water or oil perhaps) was a painting of a snake (which has not survived since its discovery in the early 1800s). As you well know by now, paintings of snakes were extremely common in the ancient town, since they were thought to tap into the power of the protective spirits of the place.

The other feature of note is no longer in its original position. It originally sat within the wall cavity above the oven. It now resides in the "secret room" of the National Archaeology Museum in Naples, where children are only permitted to enter if they are accompanied by an adult. It was another phallic symbol, embedded within a plaster frame. Within the frame were the words Hic habitat felicitas, or "Happiness lives here." The combination of the two protective symbols (the snake and the phallus) gave the baker hope that his business would survive the onslaught of invading evils.

A reproduction of how the oven was found (based on a 19th century drawing)

Protective symbols were not all that the baker relied on to ensure what might have been a profitable business. Besides selling his loaves in the front shop, this baker (along with most other bakers in the town) probably had slaves or children who served as ambulatory sellers, walking throughout the town selling loaves from shoulder bags. Perhaps their best location was the busy Forum nearby.

Leave the bakery from the western door (6.6.17), and walk northwest keeping the water tank/fountain outside that doorway to your right. Follow the street up to the northwest gate of the town. (And notice the phallus between entryways 6.17.3 and 6.17.4 — they are everywhere in this ancient town!) Your next location, the tombs of the Herculaneum Gate, is just past the town gate.

Location 34: The Tombs beyond the Herculaneum Gate

The northwest gate of the town is today referred to simply as the Herculaneum Gate, since the ancient town of Herculaneum would have been accessed through this gate and along the sea coast. In the first century, this gate was known as "the Salt Gate." Wagons passed through the middle of the gate, with pedestrians on either side. In first-century Italy, traffic was to move along the right-hand side of the road in places where streets could permit two-way traffic.

Tombs of the dead appear in significant number beyond the Herculaneum Gate. Roman law did not permit the dead to be buried within urban centers, so they are usually found in necropolises beyond the urban gates. Although there are tombs beyond other gates of Pompeii as well, these are some of Pompeii's most impressive tombs, along with those beyond the Nuceria Gate in the south (which you'll see in Tour 7, at the end of the day).

Many funerary urns holding the ashes of the deceased were found in Pompeii's tombs. Unlike the houses of Pompeii, the tombs vary greatly in their construction and appearance. When devising new funerary monuments, the individuals represented here expressed their identities in ways that was not possible when inheriting residential spaces whose architectural structures had been built in previous generations.

One tomb to notice in particular is the "seat tomb" of Mamia. You will see it on the left almost immediately after passing through the Herculaneum Gate. The expansive circular bench dedicated in Mamia's honor has a Latin inscription all along its back supports. With only the second letter now missing (and a few abbreviated spellings), the inscription reads: MAMIAE P F SACERDOTI PUBLICAE LOCUS SEPULTUR(AE) DATUS DECURIONUM DECRETO, or "To [the memory of] Mamia, daughter of Publius [Mamius], a public priestess. A place for burial was given by a decree of the town council."

Four of the five letters of the name "Mamia" deeply incised in the bench tomb dedicated to her

Mamia had been an important public benefactor in life, so the town council honored her with this tomb in her honor in order to stir up others to emulate her efforts on behalf of Pompeii. A much larger seat tomb is found beyond the Nuceria Gate and it too honors a highly influential woman of Pompeii —

Eumachia, whose building and statue you have already encountered in the south of the Forum. Perhaps there was a line of emulation that went from one of these women to the other. And as benefactors in life, so they were benefactors in perpetuity, allowing travelers to rest for a while before entering Pompeii.

If a tomb region (or necropolis) was a place of respect for those who had benefitted the town (usually the elite and their households), it was also a place that might have caused concern among some of Pompeii's residents. In the ancient imagination, tombs could be thought of as places where evil spirits lurked.

A Jewish-Christian text from the second or early third century captures this fear of evil spirits that make tombs their place of abode. In the text (Testament of Solomon 17:1-3), a demonic spirit is allowed to speak for itself. It identifies itself as "a lecherous spirit of a giant man who died in a massacre in the age of giants," and the spirit explains its strategy this way:

I seat myself near dead men in the tombs and at midnight I assume the form of the dead; if I seize anyone, I immediately kill him with the sword. If I should not be able to kill him, I cause him to be possessed by a demon and to gnaw his own flesh to pieces and the saliva of his jowls to flow down.

Pretty horrible stuff! This association of evil spirits and tombs of the dead is evident in other ancient literature as well. If Pompeians shared this fear of evil spirits lurking in the tombs, we can imagine that perhaps some would have chosen not to frequent this area after nightfall.

Archaeologists found in this area a ledge protruding from a wall, with the benevolent snake (or protective spirit of the area) painted next to it, in the hope of warding off evil from this area. Unfortunately, this demonstration of the ancient imagination has not survived.

During the hours of daylight, however, things would have been different. This is demonstrated by the number of shops that lined the street, especially on the right as you walk beyond the Herculaneum Gate.

Keep walking down the street. On the left, take notice of one other tomb that deserves quick attention, depicted in the image below. This tomb was erected by a freedwoman by the name of Naevoleia Tyche, who was the wife of

Gaius Munatius Faustus, a prominent politician in Pompeii. We will learn more about these two people on Tour 7. For now, just notice the tomb and it will be recalled to you on Tour 7. (And if you can see the tomb's depiction of a woman looking out of a window at the top of the marble, that seems to be Tyche herself, whom we'll learn more about in Tour 7.)

The tomb honoring Gaius Munatius Faustus beyond the Herculaneum Gate

At the bottom of the street, you will come upon the meandering walkway that takes you to the last location of this tour, the Villa of the Mysteries.

Location 35: The Villa of the Mysteries

Besides destroying the towns of Pompeii and Herculaneum, the eruption of Mount Vesuvius also destroyed untold numbers of villas beyond the walls of these towns. These villas were sometimes places of enormous wealth worthy of a Roman elite (as in the so-called Villa A in nearby Oplontis), and others of relative simplicity, owned by viticulturists of no particular means. Barely beyond the boundaries of the town, this relatively large villa would have been owned by someone of considerable wealth, although perhaps not one of the super-wealthy of the empire.

The most intriguing aspect of this villa is "The Room of the Mysteries," which was embedded in the more opulent end of the house (i.e., away from the slaves' quarters at the back, and toward the section of the house that had splendid views of the sea). Three sides of this room are gloriously decked out with paintings that seem to illustrate the rituals of a first-century "mystery religion." The best guess is that this was a base for the orgiastic Dionysian mystery cult, and that the pictures on the wall depict stages in the initiation process. The fact that scholars still can't quite pin down what is going on in these fantastic paintings might be credited to the fact that these ancient mystery religions really were quite secretive. We really don't know what went on behind closed doors. We can see here what most of the first-century people of Pompeii were probably never invited to see.

A young woman depicted in "The Room of the Mysteries," perhaps being prepared for initiation into the mystery cult observed in the villa

Transition to Tour 6

This is the end of Tour 5. In order to move to Tour 6, retrace your steps back to the Temple of Augustan Fortuna (Location 31). At that point you have several choices as to how you might proceed. First, you could turn south and go back to the cafeteria and toilets, if you need to recharge your batteries.

Second, you could turn north, going through the Arch of Caligula (as it was mistakenly called early on, and the name simply stuck) and proceeding along the street called Via di Mercurio. This is not part of Tour 6, but there are two or three interesting residences along that street, including the House of Apollo at 7.7.23.

Third, you could simply continue eastward, keeping the Temple of Augustan Fortuna on your right. Pass the first block (6.10), and at the second block, Tour 6 starts at the entryway to the House of the Faun at 6.12.2, where you will begin the tour that explores the northern and central sections of Pompeii.

(Note: If you have 1.5 hours or less in your day, you may need to move directly to Tour 7 at this point, since you are unlikely to fit both Tour 6 and Tour 7 into the rest of your day — unless you do little else than walk the routes. Tour 7 starts back at Location 5 from Tour 1.)

Chapter 10: The North-Central Sector

This tour will broaden your experience of some of Pompeii's most important residences and civic sites. To help you orient yourself in relation to where you'll be going, two maps of the nine locations of Tour 6 are provided here.

The first six locations of Tour 6 (36 through 41)

The last three locations of Tour 6 (42 through 44)

You are now a fairly informed reader of the architecture of Pompeii, and with the basics already covered, you will be able to move along at a steady pace in this tour. If you cannot do the whole of this tour because of time constraints, then focus on Locations 36, 39, 40, and 44 (the first and last locations of the tour). There are toilets after you complete your time in Location 44.

The final leg of this tour returns you to the center of the town. The seventh tour will then take you back to the eastern entrance of Pompeii, where your visit began. If you are pressed for time and need to leave Pompeii, you can skip Tour 6 and commence with Tour 7.

Otherwise, when you are ready, Tour 6 begins at Location 37, the House of the Faun (6.12.2).

Location 36: The House of the Faun (6.12.2)

The entrance to this house advertises the Latin word HAVE, or "welcome." And from the front entrance you can see all the way to the back of the complex — demonstrating the splendor of the household as the eye falls along a rich and varied environment. From front to back, the eye catches sight of the atrium, the tablinum (or office), the front garden, a sitting room, and finally a large columned peristyle with a second garden within it. Much of the artwork, the jewelry, the silver drinking vessels and kitchenware on display in the National Archaeology Museum in Naples originate from this house, which was one of the largest of Pompeii.

The house, the largest in Pompeii, is named after the dancing faun decoration that stood in the house's main impluvium (with a replica standing there today; the original is in the National Archaeology Museum in Naples). As you walk through the house, notice in particular two of the floor patterns. In the tablinum, you'll find a geometric pattern (using white, grey, and black) that is almost hypnotic in effect. In the sitting room, you'll find a recreation of a mosaic of Alexander the Great's defeat of the Persian king Darius in the Battle of Issus in 333 BCE. That mosaic, almost 9 feet by 17 feet in size, consists of over one and a half million pieces!

Alexander the Great, depicted in a mosaic in the House of the Faun

The eastern side of the house (to the right as you enter) was a separate section for the large number of slaves that attended to this household. As you can see, the second atrium in the eastern (slaves') section of the house has suffered considerable amounts of damage. This damage was due to bombs dropped in 1943 during World War 2.

Notice that a shrine was placed in the slaves' section of the house (to be precise, in the kitchen; you'll be able to see it if you scan the slave's section of the house, looking toward the northeast). One theory is that the household may have honored its deities in the slaves' section in order to ensure that the household's piety was in alignment from the head of the household all the way down to the humblest slave.

The shrine in the servants' quarters of the House of the Faun

At the back northwest corner of the house, in the back of the peristyle, the house had two other niches that probably housed deities or ancestors of the household. These devotional shrines ensured that the household's piety was on public display to the guests who would have walked around the peristyle while enjoying the householder's generosity at dinner parties.

If you are able to exit at the back of the house (through the northeast doorway at 6.12.7), then do, turning right as you exit. To get to the next location, walk past the first intersection and turn left at the second. (Just before that, notice a system of lead pipes on the northeast corner of block 6.13; these pipes took water from the local water tank to the houses in this region). The next location is the first door on the left.

If you are not able to exit at the back of the House of the Faun (sometimes the back exit is closed), then exit at the front where you initially entered. Turn left as you leave the house, walk past the first intersection, and turn left at the second (right after 6.13.7). After 6.13.16, carry on north to the next block, and the next location is the first door on the left.

Location 37: The House of the Vettii (6.15.1)

This was the house of two brothers of the Vetti family, named Restitutus and Conviva. Their names appear on notices on the outside walls of the house and on two stamp rings near the strongbox, making it highly likely that this is one of the few residences in Pompeii whose owners can be named.

These Vettii brothers had been born as slaves, but they earned their freedom and then rose to social prominence through economic investments that made them hefty profits. (They were, then, members of the Augustales, as discussed in Tour 7 below.) Their house, which is rich in paintings, is usually closed to the public, but its most famous feature is evident to all in the main entryway. You will see, without much effort, the exceedingly generous depiction of the deity Priapus. He seems to be weighing the riches of the house on one side of a weight-scale and balancing those riches with the weight of his enormous penis on the other side. This painting advertised the current opulence of the former slave brothers, while also enhancing the security within the house, since this deity was being called upon to act as its patron. A large strongbox for the household's money stood front and center in the atrium just beyond the entryway, placing the brothers' riches in the forefront for all to see.

Priapus depicted at the entrance of the House of the Vettii (here, only above the waist)

To get to the next location, continue north to the top of the street.

Location 38: The Vesuvian Gate

This gate into Pompeii is named after the mountain that it is oriented towards: Mount Vesuvius. In the earthquake of 62/63, this gate was largely destroyed, and the damage was still unrepaired at the time of the eruption in 79.

There are three things to notice about this gate complex. First, the most important water feature for the whole of Pompeii resides at this gate. Notice the square structure built into the western side of the gate (just beyond 5.15.18, 6.16.22 and 6.16.23). This building with three arches in its facade was the water intake reservoir that fed the whole of the town with water from the springs of Serino (in the Avellino province of Italy). Dating from the time of emperor Augustus, this reservoir collected the incoming water and channeled it into three different streams that, flowing downhill throughout the town, could be regulated according to need. One stream fed the houses of the elite; another fed the public baths; another fed the public street fountains. It is well worth peeking through the doorway at the left of the reservoir and the little outlets near the ground at the front, in order to see the three channels and the interior construction of the reservoir. Notice also the figures painted above the water intake channel. These were probably meant to represent a river deity and three nymphs.

The water intake resevoir at the Vesuvian Gate

The second thing to notice is the presence of some beautiful tombs just beyond the town gate. One of them honors a woman named Septumia, and her tomb inscription reads: "To Septumia, daughter of Lucius. Granted by decree of the town councilors a burial place and 2,000 sesterces for the funeral. Antistia Prima, daughter of Publius, her daughter, built (this monument)." Once again, the material remains of Pompeii reveal another influential woman.

Notice also the presence of another bench tomb, like the one honoring Mamia beyond the Herculaneum Gate. Once again it was a woman who was honored in this tomb's original inscription (no longer present). She was Arellia Tertulla, the daughter of Numerius and the wife of Veius Fronto. The inscription noted that "the town council gave a burial place to her after her death and decreed a funeral at public expense."

The other tomb of interest stands under a roof and is dedicated as follows: "To Gaius Vestorius Priscus, Aedile. He lived 22 years. His burial place was granted along with 2,000 sesterces for his funeral by decree of the town councilors. Mulvia Prisca, his mother, set this up at [her own] expense." Here, a mother has tried to immortalize her son, who had already risen to high ranks in the civic administration by his twenty-second year of life.

Reentering the town through the Vesuvian Gate, the third thing to notice is the painting on the left, on the path near to 5.6.19. The painting depicted two benevolent serpents moving toward offerings on an altar. Once again, the fear of evil was being tamed by belief in benevolent spirits of the place. Onto this shrine someone had painted in a rectangle a phrase to any person who chose to defecate in this place. The inscription translates as follows: "Defecator, you can hold it long enough to pass by this place."

When you are ready to pass by this place, continue southward with block 6.16 on your right and block 5.6 on your left. You are walking along the street that modern archaeologists have named Via Stabiana — or as I'll call it from now on, the Stabian Way. Carry along that street until you come to your next location at 6.16.7.

Location 39: The House of the Golden Cupids (6.16.7)

There is a good chance that this house belonged to the extended family of the second wife of emperor Nero, Poppaea Sabina (who was mentioned briefly in relation to Location 12 above, the House of Menander). Poppaea came from a political family with a mixed history of success. She seems to have had shrewd political ambitions of her own, enabling her to become the mistress of Nero in the early 60s, even while he was married to Octavia. After murdering both his mother and his wife, Nero married Poppaea in 62, perhaps the same year that the earthquake struck the area (or a year prior to it, if the disaster occurred in 63). The marriage of Nero and Poppaea was a real boon for the people of Pompeii, who benefitted from her initiatives of benefaction for the city. A handful of inscriptions from the first half of the 60s demonstrate that a fan club for Poppaea had a strong presence within Pompeii. (A graffito saluting Poppaea and written by someone named Campulus was found within the entrance of this house, and other graffiti elsewhere in the town exhibited the same sentiment.) Unfortunately, the situation that benefitted Pompeii was only short-lived, with the sudden death of Poppaea in the year 65.

Various traditions blame Nero for causing her death, while in a fit of rage against her — despite the fact that she was pregnant with his child.

The real point of interest in this house are the two shrines that adorn the four-sided peristyle in the center of the residence. The first to be seen is a fine example of a relatively ordinary household shrine, where the main deities and ancestors of the household would have been worshipped. The other is a painted shrine, dedicated to the goddess Isis — whose temple you encountered on Tour 2 (Location 13). According to Egyptian mythology, Isis resurrected her husband Osiris after he had been murdered and cut into pieces by his brothers. For her devotees, Isis promised an enhanced life in the present and eternal life after death. In the aftermath of the earthquake of 62/63, devotion to Isis was spreading like wildfire throughout Pompeii.

Plan of the House of the Golden Cupids, including the placement of two impressive household shrines

When you are ready to move on, continue walking south, keeping block 6.16 and then 6.14

on your right. Once again, notice the protective phallus adorning entryway 6.14.28. Our next location is a bit further down and on the left, at 5.1.26.

Location 40: The House of Jucundus (5.1.26)

This is another house whose owner wanted his household to be protected by the canine spirit. Notice the resting dog in the main entrance. (Think of the old adage, "It is best to let sleeping dogs lie.") We know the name of the person who owned this residence from the wax tablets found here. There were 153 wax tablets stored in this house, recording the business transactions overseen by the auctioneer-banker Lucius Caecilius Jucundus.

Although the resting dog sits at the main entrance to the residence, move to the left (north) entrance and look inside, to your immediate left. There you will see the main shrine of the household, in beautiful marble. What you cannot see is the marble relief that originally stood at the top of the front and side faces of the shrine. That relief depicted the shaking of Pompeii's Temple of Jupiter during the earthquake of 62/63. With this shrine and its pictorial reminder placed right at the entryway into Jucundus's house, no one could enter or leave the house without passing this prominent display. Evidently, from the mid-60s or so right up to the eruption of 79, the religious devotion of Jucundus's household was fashioned with specific reference to the earthquake and the fragility of life that it impressed upon the minds of Pompeii's residents.

A reconstruction of the shrine at the entrance of the House of Jucundus, with the earthquake of 62/63 depicted at the top

When you are ready to move on, continue south. When you arrive at the intersection where block 5.1 on the left meets 9.4, turn left. You can now do one of two things.

Option 1: If you have a few minutes to spare, and if you enjoy Vesuvian art, you might decide to visit the House of Marcus Lucretius Fronto. It has a lot of interesting art still in situ on the walls. The house is somewhat secluded and is often overlooked by tourists. To get there, pass blocks 5.2 and 5.3 on your left, and turn left once you pass 5.3 (keeping 5.3 on your left and 5.4 on your right). The first entrance on your right is known as 5.4.a (an unusual enumeration). When you are done there, retrace your steps along 5.3 and 5.2, until you arrive at block 9.4 on your left.

Option 2: Simply move to the next main location, which is on the right, at block 9.4.

Location 41: The Central Baths (9.4)

These baths, which are rarely open to the twenty-first century public, owe their origins to the time after the earthquake of 62/63. But even by the time of the eruption in 79, they were still not fully functioning and, consequently, were never opened to the first-century public.

Unlike most bathing complexes, there were no provisions to separate men and women in these baths. Probably the women would have been expected to bathe in the morning, prior to the arrival of the men at around noon, when the women would have been expected to vacate the premises.

Truth be told, there isn't much to see at this site, but there is still much to be learned about Pompeii from this location. In fact, it holds a key to an important aspect of Pompeii's life in the years between the earthquake and the eruption. To see the point most noticeably, go to the street that leads south between block 9.4 and block 9.5.

The odd thing here is the way that the Central Baths of block 9.4 encroach into the street, swallowing up half of the original street. Long before the eruption of 62/63, two stepping stones had been laid in the middle of the street in order to connect the pavements between block 9.4 and block 9.5. But the Central Baths of 9.4 clearly overstep the original pavement. In essence, the footprint of the building has been extended five or six feet beyond its original boundary, resulting in a marked reduction in the size of this north-south street on the eastern side of the baths. Much the same happened on the street to the south as well.

The encroachment of the Central Baths onto the street between block 9.4 and block 9.5

What seems to have happened is this. The earthquake probably destabilized buildings within block 9.4 in a fairly concentrated fashion. The town council must have decided not only to demolish the whole block but also to build a new and impressive bathing complex in that location. The location itself was ideal — a flat piece of land that would easily have benefitted from the relative proximity of the water reservoir just up the street (at Location 38).

The point of all this pertains to what was happening within the town between the earthquake and the eruption. Some have postulated that the earthquake introduced Pompeii to a sustained period of economic depression, with the town losing its vibrancy and going into a period of steady decline. A few aspects of the town's life could be interpreted in that way (such as the slow rebuilding of some of its traditional temples). But a number of indicators suggest that scenarios of depression are dubious. The Central Baths is one of those indicators. Demolishing a town block in order to erect an impressive huge new bathing complex runs contrary to models of decline.

To move to the next location, continue south along the Stabian Way (with block 9.4 on your left) until you arrive at block 9.2 (again, on your left). Along the way, if the House of Lucretius is open (at 9.3.5) and if time permits, you might enjoy some of its artwork in situ.

Location 42: The Neighborhood Shrine (9.2.1)

As you arrive at the intersection where block 9.2 is ahead of you and to your left, you will notice how the structure at 9.2.1 engulfs the pedestrian pavement along the eastern side of the Stabian Way. That structure has been allowed to overshoot the construction footprint normally expected for buildings.

The neighborhood shrine at 9.2.1

This structure was a sizeable neighborhood shrine — the largest neighborhood shrine in Pompeii. In fact, you have now entered a region in which neighborhood shrines of various kinds were highly concentrated. (Some of these shrines were in the streets along the back of these properties and, consequently, they are not currently accessible to tourists.)

It isn't clear why this area benefitted from a higher proportion of neighborhood shrines than any other in Pompeii. Was this an especially dangerous neighborhood? Were leading figures in this neighborhood particularly interested in enhancing the spiritual dynamics of the neighborhood that they lived in? Was the high concentration of public shrines in this neighborhood simply a coincidence? We will never know the answer to these questions, but they are intriguing to consider nevertheless.

One particular feature of this shrine resonates with architectural features in high concentration elsewhere within this neighborhood. As you look eastward toward 9.2.1 while standing on the Stabian Way, you see the feature embedded on the third lava stone from the bottom on the left pillar (the pillar's inner stone). The phallus (in this case, pointing south along the Stabian Way) is not something you would normally want to highlight, but you are touring Pompeii, where local residents saw in it the power of life, luck, and protection. You have seen this symbol so many times already today. You'll also see the same symbol as you continue south to your next location.

To get to our next location, continue south along the Stabian Way until you rejoin the Street of Abundance. Along the way, try to spot one more neighborhood shrine and several more phalluses. (For the shrine, see the niche in the south wall of 9.2, between 9.2 and 9.1. For phalluses, look first between entryways for 9.2.6 and 9.2.7, and then, on the next block on the left, between entryways for 9.1.13 and 9.1.14.)

Location 43: Holconius's Arch on the Street of Abundance (between 7.1.12 and 8.4.17)

You have now returned to the Street of Abundance, which you know so well from Tour 1. This point was one of the main crossroads of the town. Here, a sizeable four-sided arch stood over the Street of Abundance. Although most of the structure has not survived, you can still find the bases of the pillars standing at this important crossroad.

Since this was a main point of traffic through the town, it comes as no surprise that the arch was dedicated to one of Pompeii's most distinguished citizens. You have already seen this citizen honored elsewhere in the town — in particular, in the Large Theater, where the location of his seat was embedded in the marble in a central position, so that all could see him. Remember Holconius?

www.ingramcontent.com/pod-product-compliance
Lightning Source LLC
Chambersburg PA
CBHW050024130526
44590CB00042B/1876